PRAYING THE SCRIPTURES

To my ever-supportive parents,
Christy and Breda,
I dedicate this book
with gratitude and affection.

CHRISTOPHER HAYDEN

Praying the Scriptures

A practical introduction to
Lectio Divina

ST PAULS

ACKNOWLEDGEMENTS

I would like to offer my thanks to the following individuals: Annabel Robson, Commissioning Editor at ST PAULS Publishing in London, for the invitation to write this book; J.K., who insisted that I accept the invitation; John Dutto I.M.C., who introduced me to *lectio divina*; Francis Davidson, who gave encouragement and help with the manuscript.

Cover Image: *The Risen Christ*,
Demetz art studio, Ortisei, Italy
Used with permission

ST PAULS Publishing
187 Battersea Bridge Road, London SW11 3AS, UK
www.stpauls.ie

ISBN 085439 587 3

Set by TuKan DTP, Fareham, UK
Printed by The Guernsey Press Co. Ltd., Guernsey, C.I.

ST PAULS is an activity of the priests and brothers
of the Society of St Paul who proclaim the Gospel
through the media of social communication

Contents

Foreword

I know no better introduction to the life-giving practice of *lectio divina*. With clarity and skill, Fr Hayden uses the Gospel of Mark as a guide for those who wish to pray the Scriptures. This book should encourage many to absorb carefully and live the Scriptures.

Gerald O'Collins, S.J.
Professor of Systematic Theology,
Gregorian University, Rome

Introduction

'Lord, teach us to pray.' This was the plea addressed to Jesus by his disciples, immediately after they had seen him at prayer (Lk 11:1)[1]. Their plea was already a prayer, and a most effective one. The very words 'Lord, teach us to pray' suggest that it is only through prayer that we can learn to pray. To want to learn to pray is to be confronted with a kind of divine catch-22: the only person from whom we can truly learn to pray is the one to whom we wish to pray! We learn to pray by praying.

This little book will not teach you to pray. Were it a much larger book, it could not do that. Perhaps the most that any book or guide can aspire to is to provide a few pointers and some encouragement. Prayer, as we will see, is about a relationship with God. Indeed, it *is* a relationship with God. By definition, a relationship is something which must be *entered into*. No amount of information about a person, no amount of biographies read and studied, constitute a relationship with the person concerned. Theory regarding prayer may be useful, and good practice generally flows from good ideas; but when it comes to prayer, there is simply no substitute for praying.

Given this waiver, it might be in order to state

just what the aim of this book is. We will explore something of the relationship between the Bible (or 'Scripture'), as the word of God, and prayer, as a response to God and an entering into relationship with him. We are well used to hearing the expression, 'This is the word of the Lord,' when the readings are proclaimed in church. If the Bible is indeed God's word, then it follows that it has a unique importance for those who wish to pray. The beginning of a relationship is getting to know someone, and we do this primarily by listening. But what does it mean to listen to God's word? And what is God's word, as we find it in the Bible, about?

Practically every Christian has some basic ideas regarding prayer and Scripture: prayer is an activity of such and such a kind – the Bible is this or that kind of book. The reality is that while many of our basic ideas may be correct, some of them may be imprecise, and others downright flawed. Therefore, our first task will be to gain some clarity regarding what prayer and the Bible are – and what they are not. This concern will guide the first part of this book.

As we have already suggested, prayer and Scripture are connected to each other in a special way. Our efforts to pray, to enter into and remain in a relationship with God, need to have their roots in the Bible. The Bible is more than just a guide for our prayer, or a collection of texts that can help us to pray. It contains the word of God to which prayer is our response. In the second part of the book we will try to draw prayer and Scripture together. Any worthwhile task or project which we undertake benefits from being approached with a clear method rather than in a hit-and-miss fashion. Accordingly, we will look at a specific method for praying the Scriptures. This method, which is as practical as it is ancient, is known as *lectio divina*. In spite of the Latin title, there is nothing mysterious or esoteric about it. In fact, we shall see that *lectio divina* is simplicity itself. While it is far from being an automatic 'recipe' for praying with the Scriptures, it can give a helpful structure or framework to our prayer.

It is said that there is nothing as practical as a good theory, and while we will try to avoid being too theoretical in any of our exploration, it might help to consolidate our reflections if we end with a sustained, practical exercise in *lectio divina*. The last part of the book will consist of a short, reflective introduction to the Gospel of Mark, and a prayerful reading of some passages from Mark, using the method and insights of *lectio divina*.

Part One

Prayer and Scripture

What prayer is

Those who were brought up on the older Catechism will be familiar with the idea that prayer is 'the raising of the heart and mind to God.' While this definition is by no means incorrect, it has the potential to be slightly misleading. 'To God' is a very long way for the small and probably distracted human mind and heart to raise themselves! Insofar as we raise – or attempt to raise – our minds and hearts to God, we do so as a response to the God who has already reached down to us; the God who, in his Son Jesus, has already bridged the infinite distance between the creator and his creatures.

Our response to the God who has spoken first

Prayer naturally involves our initiative, but only as a response to a prior initiative. Prayer is *our response to the God who has spoken first*. To insist on this is more than simply a question of getting the theory right. It means that when we pray, we are doing nothing other than opening up to the God who is already in communication with us. Scripture tells us that God *is* communication: 'In the beginning was the word'

(Jn 1:1). God does not sit in some splendid, silent isolation. It is his very nature to be in communication with his creation. He does not need to be 'activated,' or pestered into concern for his creatures. Jesus told the parable of the importunate widow (Lk 18:1-8), in order to make the point that God is *not* like the judge in the story, who needed a lot of persuasion before responding to someone in need.

Trusting that to pray is simply to turn to our Father who has begun the dialogue has a further happy consequence. Our prayer need not be an anxious stream of words; we need not come up with the right phrase, the best formulation. We can be free of the compulsion to pile sentences one on top of the other, or to brow-beat God by force of repetition. In fact, few enough words are needed, and the few that may be necessary are for our own sake, not for God's. Jesus himself was aware of the tendency to 'over-pray,' and so he instructed his disciples: 'When you are praying, do not heap up empty phrases as the Gentiles do; for they think that they will be heard because of their many words. Do not be like them, for your Father knows what you need before you ask him' (Mt 6:7).

Of course, there are times when we feel a desperate need to 'storm heaven'. Usually, at such times, we are acutely anxious about a loved one. It may be that our prayer then seems no different to the anxious babbling that Jesus discouraged in his followers. However, even a stream of words may flow from the depths of our heart, and be a deep expression of our trust in the Lord. It is for our calmer moments that we may need a reminder that God does not require us to shout at him in prayer. Humble trust, rather than anxious or compulsive repetition, is the key to communication with our loving Father.

Our search for the God who has already found us

Prayer, then, is our response to the God who has already spoken to us. But God has done so much more than speak. From the very beginning of the Bible, it is clear that God's word is not simply declarative, it is creative. God speaks not just in order to pass things on, but in order to bring things to pass. In the opening verses of the book of Genesis, we read several times: 'God said... and it was so.' God's words are matched by his providence, his infinitely wise guidance of all events in history. For every passage in Scripture which speaks to us of God's love, we can be sure that there is an invisible network of providence at work in our lives. St Paul expressed this conviction that God's care for his creatures pervades all of reality, when he wrote: 'We know that all things work together for good for those who love God' (Rom 8:28).

God's providence is not some anonymous 'force,' calculated to keep creation running smoothly. It is his love at work in creation, a love which is deeply personal, and which encounters each of us in an individual and personal way. Just as God has spoken his word before we begin to speak to him, in the same way his love has reached us before we begin to reach out to him. God is the one who has 'chosen us in Christ before the foundation of the world' (Eph 1:4). Very often, our prayer is a conscious –

and perhaps agonised – reaching out to God, in an attempt to grasp his presence, to know the reality of God in our lives. Once again, God is there ahead of us. He chose us before we were aware of him; his providence guides us, even when we are not aware of it. Insofar, then, as our prayer is a search for God, it is *our search for the God who has already found us*. St Augustine long ago expressed this when he prayed, after his conversion: 'You were with me; I was not with you.' The writer of Psalm 139 was imbued with a similar sense of God's providence: 'O Lord, you have searched me and known me... You search out my path and my lying down... Even before a word is on my tongue, O Lord, you know it completely' (vv. 1, 3, 4).

Our commitment to the God who has loved us first

Prayer is more than words. We have seen that the words we use are, in themselves, of secondary importance, whereas the attitude behind the words is what matters. Many of us were brought up on prayers which were called 'acts' – acts of faith, hope and charity. Imagine the effectiveness of an uttered 'act of charity' without any deed or 'action' of charity to confirm it? Such a spoken 'act' would be rendered null and void by inaction. It would as debased as banknotes printed without any gold bullion to back them up. Jesus leaves us in no doubt about this, when he says: 'Not everyone who says to me, "Lord, Lord," will enter the kingdom of heaven, but only the one who does the will of my Father in heaven' (Mt 7:21). Prayer and action are completely inseparable. The words, groans and aspirations which make up our prayer need to translate into the warp and woof of our daily living.

Of course, prayer *can* be separated from life, but if it is, it is hollow and inauthentic. In the Old Testament, the prophets railed against those who thought that worship of God was a matter of formula and precept, while forgetting about the commitment of life which needed to accompany it. At the beginning of the book of Isaiah, God condemns prayer which is not matched by life: 'When you stretch out your hands, I will hide my eyes from you; even though you make many prayers, I will not listen' (Is 1:15). What is needed in order for prayer to be acceptable to God? 'Wash yourselves; make yourselves clean; remove the evil of your doings from before my eyes; cease to do evil, learn to do good' (Is 1:16). The measure of our prayer is our life. People often express misgivings about the quality of their prayer: 'I can't pray,' 'I feel nothing when I pray.' But, to repeat, the measure of our prayer is our life, not our feelings. If our life is marked by a sincere effort to love others, to forgive, to endure patiently, then we can be sure that our prayer, however it may feel, is not far wide of the mark.

What all of this amounts to is that our prayer should be a reflection of our Christian commitment. The God who has spoken first, who has already reached out to us, has called us 'to be holy and blameless before him in love' (Eph 1:4). Prayer is therefore *our commitment to the God who has loved us first*. St John puts this very succinctly in his first letter: 'We love because he first loved us' (1 Jn 4:19); and again, 'Those who love God must love their brothers and sisters also' (v. 21). Here, we touch not only on the nature of prayer, but on the nature – indeed the essence – of Christian morality. Living the 'good' Christian life is not about keeping the rules and thus winning favour with God. It is nothing other than living a life of gratitude to the God who has already shown us favour. God's favour, given freely to us, is the foundation of all Christian moral living. Sadly, it is all too often thought that God's favour is the prize which Christian morality tries to win. The reality is that God *only* loves. He leaves to his creatures the choice of how to respond to his love. Christian prayer and living are our concrete, committed, grateful response to the love of God.

This is a key point for our prayer with the Bible. Large sections of the Bible recount God's free choice of his people, and their varied and varying response to that choice. For the moment, let us remember that nothing in our lives as Christians is, properly speaking, our initiative. All our praying and acting is done against the background of what God has already done for us. We are called to make our lives a 'thank you' and a 'yes' to the initiative and plan of God. Mary, the great disciple, is the model of this attitude: 'Let it be with me according to your word' (Lk 1:38). Even at the height of his work of preaching and evangelising, St Paul could say: 'All this is from God' (2 Cor 5:18). Our life itself is from God. We, the creatures, cannot return the favour to our Creator. Instead we are called to return thanks. This is the essence of Christian prayer and living: a grateful response to the loving initiative of God.

Our trustful openness to letting God's plan take root in our lives

Everything we have said so far about prayer and discipleship is rooted in *faith*. We cannot pick up a copy of God's plan for us, and simply read it off. We can have no direct sense experience of God's initiative in our lives. God is *transcendent*, beyond our limited capacity to reason and understand. Through the centuries, many saints and mystics have said that when we draw close to God, we actually experience his infinite light as darkness, because we are unable to grasp him with our minds. The fact that God is so completely beyond us means that we need to approach him with great *trust*. We will never understand God. We will never – at least in this life – understand his workings. The experiences of our lives will sometimes point clearly towards the workings of a loving Father, but at other times they will appear to point in the opposite direction. Our lives, the world, simultaneously *reveal* and *conceal* the presence of God. Our need for trust is never greater than when God appears absent; when, in spite of all that we believe, we can see no sign of God.

God – we believe – has a plan for our lives. At times, our task may be not so much to *discern* this plan, as to live in trust that God is leading us. Even the appearance of chaos does not negate God's plan. At times in our lives, we may be able to discern in hindsight how God was at work in a hidden or surprising way, but in general, the only 'experience' of God's plan available to us lies in trusting faith. Perhaps not surprisingly, one of the loveliest assurances in the Bible of God's plans for his people dates from a time when their trust in God had been shaken by bitter experience. The prophet Jeremiah had seen his people suffer deeply as a result of their neglect of God and their forgetfulness of the values by which God had called them to live. Jeremiah was confident that God had not rejected his chosen people, but was still intent on blessing them according to the plans he had for them: 'For surely I know the plans I have for you, says the Lord, plans for your welfare and not for harm, to give you a future with hope' (Jer 29:11).

As human beings, a good deal of our attention and energy tends to focus on our 'plans' – our hopes, dreams and intentions, which we often pursue with the best of faith. Part of the long road to Christian maturity is growth in the realisation that our plans – good though they may be – are not necessarily God's plans. Furthermore, we are invited to the startling realisation that God's plans are even better than our own! Thus, as life progresses, prayer becomes increasingly *our trustful openness to letting God's plan take root in our lives*. The dream of an ordinary fisherman might have been to become a great fisherman. The dream of a successful rabbi might have been to become the greatest rabbi. But God's plans were greater still. The Bible is peopled with examples of how God's plans exceeded human expectation and desire. In every case, what was required from the human point of view was *trust*.

This will be another key point when we turn our attention to the Bible. There we find the story of God's plan for his people, unfolding gradually through fidelity and betrayal, frustration and success.

God's plan is never thwarted by human weakness or misunderstanding; nor, paradoxically, is it particularly helped by human talent or brilliance. The only human ingredient upon which its successful implementation might almost be said to depend is trust. Trust and faith are very closely linked. In the language of the Bible, they are often one and the same word. Faith is in our minds, to the extent that it involves belief in certain facts, but it is also in our hearts, where it is lived out as trust in God.

'All this is from God,' to quote Paul once again. Prayer is completely rooted in God's initiative. In trying to understand this, we have done more than just outline what prayer is about; we have in fact touched on what it means to be a Christian. Just what is a Christian? Our familiarity with the term may breed a certain lack of clarity. Sometimes we may even use the term 'Christian' to describe people who have no faith, but whom we consider to be upright and decent people. However, the term 'Christian' is not a value-judgement. Christians do not have a monopoly on uprightness and decency, any more than non-Christians have a monopoly on 'unchristian' behaviour.

Fundamentally, a Christian is someone who is convinced of the reality of God's loving initiative, which has reached its highest expression in Jesus. He or she is not so much someone who does things for God, but who is convinced, like Mary, that 'the Mighty One has done great things for me' (Lk 1:49). Therefore, Christian living is nothing other than a *response* to the love of God revealed in Christ, and a continued openness to his initiative. When we approach the Bible, we do so with openness and with the desire to respond to God's word. For the Christian, Scripture and prayer are two sides of a single coin, as closely related as God's initiative and our response.

What prayer is not

In practice, times of prayer are often long struggles to leave aside distractions, so that we can simply sit in God's presence, listening to him rather than to the myriad voices within ourselves. On the level of our understanding also, we might do well to spend a few moments leaving aside some imprecise or misleading notions regarding prayer. Correctly understood, prayer can clearly be seen as something healthy and life-giving. Some of the difficulties and discouragements which we face in prayer may result from misconceptions or wrong expectations. Let us identify a few such wrong ideas, so that we may become more free of them.

Not an attempt to manipulate or change God

The first caution applies most clearly to the prayer of petition or intercession, in which we bring our needs and the needs of others to God. It is that prayer is not an attempt to manipulate or change God. Nobody who prays sincerely would think of it in this way, and yet our prayer is often calculated – perhaps quite unconsciously – to set God on the straight and narrow. We have clear and sincere ideas of what is best, and God has the power to implement them for us. There is nothing at all wrong about bringing specific requests and petitions to God in prayer. On the contrary, we are asked to do just that: 'By prayer and supplication with thanksgiving let your requests be made known to God' (Phil 4:6). However, we discover sooner or later (generally much sooner!) that prayer most often does not work in a direct or 'automatic' way. This can be a cause of great suffering to us, even of scandal to our faith in a loving God.

Imagine for a moment if prayer *were* automatically effective, and we 'got what we asked for' all of the time. How long would it be before God became indistinguishable from a genie, and prayer indistinguishable from rubbing the magic lamp? What would become of the attitude of trust and hope in God? And this might be only the beginning of our woes. Our perspective on things is limited; our understanding partial. How many opportunities for growth and depth might be squandered on quick-fix solutions? How long would our openness to mystery survive if we could find quick refuge from the pains and storms of life? There is no simple answer to the problem of unanswered prayer, and there will always be times when the silence or inaction of God will seem frankly scandalous. But our faith tells us to keep on praying, praying to the God whose hand we cannot force, whose mind we cannot change.

What happens when we remain faithful to prayer, in spite of delay or disappointment? We gradually come to the realisation that our prayer changes not God, but us. It is we ourselves who are changed by prayer. It is we who gain a new perspective and a new openness. We may not understand the workings of God, we might still choose some things differently, but we come to appreciate gradually that the Lord knows what he is about: 'My thoughts are not your thoughts, nor are your ways my ways, says the Lord. For as the heavens are higher than the earth, so are my ways higher than your ways and my thoughts higher than your thoughts' (Is 55:8-9).

This realisation does not come easily, but only after a time of wrestling with God in prayer. If we pray only sporadically, or when our back is to the wall, we are unlikely to reach it. The figure of Jacob in the Old Testament, wrestling at night with a being whom he did not recognise, is often used as an image of the struggle to persevere in prayer to the God whom we do not understand. Jacob was faithful to the struggle, and in the end he was blessed by his opponent (Gen 32:22-29). When, during the night times of life, we remain faithful to prayer, the blessing we receive may not be the one we had initially sought, but, like Jacob, we *will* be blessed for our perseverance.

Not an escapist flight from reality

One of the commoner objections to spending time in prayer is that it is not the best possible use of time, but a flight from commitment and from the problems of life. Why spend time in prayer, when we could be helping others? Why indulge ourselves with the cosiness of the chapel or the oratory, when we could be *doing* something? Why pray in a world filled with social problems, when our good deeds for others could be a most acceptable offering to God? The grain of truth in such objections is that our prayer should indeed be matched by Christian action, and if it is not, then it risks being inauthentic. However, this does not take from the value of prayer in itself.

Far from being a *fuga mundi*, a flight from the world, prayer – if it is genuine – sends us right back into the thick of things. The Bible is replete with examples of intense prayer, followed by intense activity, Jesus himself being the best example of all. Before beginning his public ministry, he made a forty-day retreat (Lk 4:1-13). He spent a night in prayer before choosing the twelve apostles (Lk 6:12-13). He took care to arrange a prayerful time with the twelve as his final hours approached (Lk 22:7-23). The apostles themselves were called to spend time with Jesus, but this was a prelude to their being 'sent out to proclaim the message' (Mk 3:14). Moses drew closer to God than any person ever had before him, but this was so that he might receive from God his life's task of leading the chosen people out of slavery and into the Promised Land (Ex 3).

God is Reality. Therefore authentic prayer cannot but plunge us into reality. Far from being an escape from reality, prayer leads us to greater clarity and commitment. Our own inertia and sinful attitudes often keep us from full and honest confrontation with reality, but they cannot hold out indefinitely against sincere prayer. Sooner or later, we must either stop praying, or become more real. Nobody can remain unreal for long in God's presence, while being confronted with God's word. How could we nurse a grudge, while consistently exposing ourselves to the presence and word of a God of forgiveness? Can we fail to be pained by dishonesty or injustice in our dealings with others, if we are in regular contact with Holiness and Goodness Itself? Since prayer purifies us (slowly, at times painfully) of our unreality, it leaves us better equipped to deal in a balanced and realistic way with our own limitations and those of the world around us. It prepares us for our mission, as baptized Christians, of bringing about the Kingdom of God in our world.

Prayer, then, is far from being a flight from reality. But it should be remembered that for God's children, there is no better *rest* from the demands and stresses of living than spending time in the presence of the Father. When we need a break, there are many healthy and wholesome forms of recreation available to us. But it is above all through prayer that we are renewed for continued service and discipleship. The depressed, burnt-out prophet Elijah found respite through time spent alone with God, after which he had the strength and enthusiasm to complete his mission (1 Kings 19). In prayer, we too can experience God's presence not only as a challenge, but also as a balm for the bruises which life sometimes inflicts on us.

Not so much about feelings as about commitment

Feelings are important! We are well aware of how important it is to respect the feelings of others, and to be 'in touch' with our own. While we know that love does not consist purely of feelings, there would be something absurd about a love devoid of feelings. When we are faced with major decisions for our lives, our deeper feelings are a fundamental guide. But we also know that our feelings are ambivalent and fickle. We cannot live our day-to-day lives by whim. Less still can we plan for the future on the basis of today's feelings. Inside, we may blow hot and cold, but life and relationships need steadiness and dependability. To be 'grown up' is to recognize this and act accordingly.

We relate to God as the human beings which he has created – feelings included. To take God seriously does not mean to deny our own humanity or any part of it. After all, we are relating to the God who took on every aspect of our human nature. However, our feelings are just as ambivalent in prayer as they are in any other aspect of our lives. For this reason we need to bear in mind that prayer is not so much a matter of feelings, as a matter of commitment. It can happen that when a person begins to pray seriously for the first time, their feelings are deeply touched. They may be filled with an awareness of the reality of God, and experience a real 'spiritual high'. This has been compared to a honeymoon, or a period of falling in love. But like the equivalent relationship between a man and a woman, the initial intensity eventually wanes. It is then time to settle down to a more steady relationship. The intensity may not always be present, but the depth can grow over a lifetime.

Many people come to equate the quality of their prayer with the strength or depth of their feelings. 'I can't pray', and 'I feel nothing when I pray', are common complaints. But prayer is based on faith conviction rather than on feelings. It is true that the absence of any feeling can be a real test of our strength and patience. There is probably nothing more difficult that to sit still when we are filled not with sweetness and light, but with the awareness of our own inner poverty. But here, as elsewhere, we need to learn that God is in control. We cannot switch his presence on as we please, but must wait patiently. If we resort to praying only when we feel like it or when it feels good, we will pray less and less, and eventually, probably not at all.

This becomes very relevant when we begin to pray with the Bible. At times, God's word will seem to jump off the page to meet us. Every verse and phrase will be filled with depths of personal meaning, as though written for nobody else. But in the ordinary run of things, we will not experience a rush of insight every time we open our Bible. We may instead have a tired sensation of *déjà vu*, when we read well-worn and often-heard passages from the Bible. At such times, we need to remember that God works on us, and his word sinks deep within us, even when we are unaware of it. The effectiveness of God's word does not depend on our mood – it is intrinsically effective: 'As the rain and snow come down from heaven, and do not return there until they have watered the earth, making it bring forth and sprout... so shall my word be that goes out from my mouth; it shall not return to me empty, but it shall accomplish that which I purpose, and succeed in the thing for which I have sent it' (Is 55:10-11). In our prayer and our reading of Scripture, we are asked not to pursue results, but to pursue fidelity. We can confidently leave the results to the One who 'gives the growth' (1 Cor 3:7).

Not so much an activity as a 'passivity'

A constant challenge to believers is to make time for prayer. This generally presents itself as the main reason why we do not pray as much as we ought. How do we make time specifically for prayer, given our hectic schedules, and the stream of activity that fills our waking hours? Granted, all that we do can and should be an offering to God; we are called to make our lives a prayer. However, in order for everything we do to be prayer, we need to ensure that there are times when we do nothing but pray. Yet for many people, the sheer business of life can sometimes leave little space to do more than respond to demands as they arise. There may be periods when any kind of recollection is effectively impossible.

Taking account of all such situations, the reality is that pressure of time is not generally the main obstacle to prayer. If we are to be perfectly frank, while time may be the *excuse*, the *reason* lies elsewhere. We find it difficult to take time out for prayer from all our activities precisely because prayer is not an activity. It is much more a 'passivity' than an activity. As we have seen, to pray is not so much to do as to wait – to wait in stillness and silence. It is very difficult indeed to remain silent. It can happen that as soon as we enter into a state of external quiet and physical stillness, we are confronted with our own inner noise and agitation. Our minds and imaginations are full, and in the absence of some external stimulation they can practically run riot. At such times it can take a mammoth effort of will simply to remain still; it can seem that nothing is more difficult to do than doing nothing! In these moments, God seems absent, and the temptation is to throw in the towel. Yet these are valuable moments. They can put us in touch with our inner poverty, and teach us our utter dependence on

God. In short, they can lead us to greater humility and trust.

We should not fear or decline the Master's invitation, issued to us as it was to the twelve apostles: 'Come away to a deserted place all by yourselves and rest a while' (Mk 6:31). The desert which we find within ourselves may be just the place where the Lord wishes to plant his word.

What the Scriptures are

What is the Bible? This might seem a rather obvious question, but in fact it is one that is well worth asking. Of course, Christians believe that the Bible is the word of God, that it is inspired, that it is revelation, but just what do these expressions mean? We will try to clarify each of them in turn, but first, let us ask about the content, or subject matter, of the Bible: What is it about? Again, this appears to be a very obvious question, but in practice the answer is not quite so obvious. Numerous biblical scholars have laboured to find a single, key idea which might do justice to the overall content of the Bible. None of them would suggest for a moment that one single idea could ever fully express the rich and varied content of the Bible, but they have been motivated by the wish to detect a reasonably compact theme that might guide our reading of, and reflection on, the Bible.

Among the many suggestions which have been made for a central, guiding idea are that the Bible deals essentially with the kingdom of God, or that its overall subject matter is God's choice of a people for himself, or that its basic concern is with God's promises to humanity. The reason for such variety is that the Bible is not a single, unified book. Rather, it is a library between two covers, made up of numerous books, written by different authors, in different situations, over a period of many centuries. This makes the Bible a complex but incredibly rich 'book'. It also makes it difficult to find a single, central thread to guide our reading of the Bible.

At the very broadest, we can say that the Bible contains a record of God's dealings with his people and reflection by his people on their relationship with him. Under this broad umbrella-heading, we can place two principal ideas: the Bible is about the history of salvation and the covenant between God and his people.

A record of God's dealings with his people

First of all, the Bible's central concern is 'salvation history'. This term was coined by scholars to describe how, in the Bible, we see God acting through history, through the ups and downs which his people experience. God's sole concern is the welfare of his people. He frees them from captivity, gives them guidance for living in peace and harmony, and provides all the material blessings they need. When his people become forgetful of him, God is able to use the events of their lives to draw them back to him. The Bible is laden with the conviction that God is in control of all the events of history. This is why history can be described as 'salvation history'. Even the most painful and distressing experiences which God's people endure can work for their salvation. Nothing – not even the sinfulness of his people – is able to thwart God's desire and ability to draw his people close to himself.

In the Old Testament, the central saving act which God worked for his people was the exodus (the event from which the second book of the Bible takes its name). In the exodus, God *saved* his people, by leading them out from slavery in Egypt, and this was only the beginning of a long journey to freedom. God's intention was that they should live in peace and freedom in the Promised Land, to which he would guide them. The conviction of God's people, expressed throughout the Bible, was that they had been saved by God, and they looked to God above all as *the one who saves*. In the New Testament, this conviction reaches its highpoint: in Jesus, *the Saviour*, God has shown the depth of his love for humanity, and the strength of his desire that all people be freed from every form of captivity.

The original exodus event became a symbol or metaphor for the ways in which God continued to intervene to protect and deliver his people. It was the foundation of the people's relationship with God and their obedience to him. The ten commandments, in Exodus 20 and Deuteronomy 5, are introduced with the words, 'I am the Lord your God, who brought you out of the land of Egypt, out of the house of slavery.' God's people owe him trustful obedience, since he has proven his care for them. The exodus was God's *initiative*, calling for a *response* on the part of his people.

For us, today, the exodus continues to be a powerful metaphor. It offers the consolation that God can work through all of the events of *our* lives to lead us from captivity to freedom (our personal history is 'salvation history'). There is nothing in *our* experience that lies beyond the merciful reach of God's providence. We also find in the exodus the ongoing challenge of fidelity to the God who calls and saves us. We are invited to make our lives a 'thank you' to our Saviour. We will see, when we begin our reflection on *lectio divina*, that an essential part of our prayer with the Bible is the effort to understand how the saving events recounted in Scripture are reflected in our own lives. To pray the Scriptures is to detect the continuity between the salvation history we read there and our own personal history.

Now to the second key idea which can help to focus our overall understanding of the Bible: that of 'covenant'. The Bible is the book of the covenant. In fact the word 'testament' has the same meaning as the word 'covenant'. In the broadest sense, 'covenant' refers to the special *relationship* between God and his people. This relationship was God's initiative but, like any relationship, was a two-sided affair. For his part, God had freely chosen his people, and rescued them from captivity. Furthermore, he promised to continue to bless them. For their part, the people were obliged to remain faithful to God, to worship him alone, and to live in the way that he had shown them. God's commandments were not an arbitrary set of rules, but were his wise guidance for his people. If the people lived by these commandments, they would be 'following the maker's instructions', and living as God intended them to live. They would be living within the covenant.

God could not and would not be unfaithful to

his people. He would never break the covenant. However, the people had to make and renew a clear, deliberate choice of fidelity to their relationship with God. They had to reject the temptation to idolatry (putting anything else in place of God), and be on guard against growing lukewarm in their commitment to God. A good starting point for their efforts to live within the covenant was the realisation that God had not chosen them because of any merit on their part, but simply because he loved them. There was therefore a special onus on the people not so much to keep a set of rules, as to express their gratitude to God for the love which he had shown: 'It was not because you were more numerous than any other people that the Lord set his heart on you and chose you – for you were the fewest of all peoples. It was because the Lord loved you' (Deut 7:7-8).

The theme of covenant, just like its sister-theme of salvation history, can speak loudly to believers today. It reminds us that the relationship between God and the believer is rooted in God's loving choice. Our response to God is a response to love, and love is the very best possible motivation for fidelity. God's covenant was not with isolated individuals, but with a *people*. Awareness of this calls us to solidarity with others, and reminds us that our relationship with God has a 'horizontal' as well as a 'vertical' dimension: it is not an individualistic, purely private, *tête-à-tête* with God.

In the Bible, the covenant relationship between God and his people is sometimes expressed by means of very personal and tender images. God is the Bridegroom, pleading for fidelity on the part of his bride (Hos 2); He is the Shepherd, caring for his sheep (Is 40:11; Ps 23); He is the owner of a vineyard which he lovingly and carefully tends (Is 5:1-7). It is in the person of Jesus that God's care for his people is most perfectly expressed. Jesus inaugurates the long hoped-for 'new covenant' (Jer 31:31-34), and fulfils the images found in the Old Testament. He is the Bridegroom, Matthew 25:1-13; the Good Shepherd, John 15:1-11; the Vinedresser, John 10:11-18. Such images remind us that the God of Scripture, the God to whom we pray, is passionate about humanity and about each individual. This is the God who calls us into relationship with himself – a God who wears his heart on his sleeve when it comes to expressing his love for people. To pray the Scriptures is to do nothing other than deepen our acquaintance with this God.

Now that we are equipped with the twin ideas of salvation history and covenant, perhaps we might venture to express, in a nutshell, what the Bible is about. It is the record of the relationship ('covenant') between God and his people. It shows us how this relationship worked itself out in the lives of God's people, and how God remained faithful to them, guiding every aspect of their history in order to draw them closer to himself ('salvation history'). In the New Testament we see how, in the person of Jesus, salvation history reaches its high point, with the inauguration of the new covenant in Jesus' blood (Mk 14:24). The Bible has very much to say to us, as we strive to deepen our own relationship with God, in the unfolding of our personal – and social – history.

The word of God in human words

The Bible is the word of God – but just what does this mean? Many people approach the Bible with the unspoken understanding that it is a book of straight-forward divine dictation, as though God had uttered every word into the ear of the writer. This would imply that people like Mark or Hosea were simply scribes, people with no more input into the writing of the biblical books than a secretary taking dictation from a great novelist. Such a view might appear to protect the belief that the Bible is the word of God, but in fact it sells God short, because it suggests that God could not take the risk of allowing any human input into the writing of Scripture.

It is not possible to be a Christian without the belief that Jesus is both God and man – fully human and fully divine. If God, in Jesus, could fully take on and work through our human nature, then it is hardly disrespectful to suggest that, in the writing of Scripture, he could fully take on and work through our human language and thought processes. This is in fact the belief of the Church, which insists that the Bible is *the word of God in human words*. Jesus, having taken on human nature to the extent of being like us in all things but sin (Heb 4:15), chose not to be free of the limitations inherent in human nature. Likewise, God, in committing his words to human language, 'risked' the limitations of human language.

This has direct consequences for the believer, who reads the Bible with faith, and with the anticipation that God will speak through his word in Scripture. Just as with any other form of human expression, we will find that the Bible is less than clear in places.

Its expressions can be obscure or ambivalent. It was written not in a vacuum, but in a particular culture and in a particular language – to us today, a foreign culture and a foreign language. Being aware of these factors may help to temper our expectations, and lead us to approach the Bible with a certain respect. It is certainly not a 'closed book,' but on the other hand, we cannot expect simply to pick it up and immediately understand all that we read. Genuine respect for the word of God demands that we approach it with the humility to acknowledge this.

Inspired

What about *inspiration*? Does what we have just said take in any way from the belief that the Bible is truly inspired by God's Holy Spirit? Not at all, given the right understanding of inspiration. The best starting point for a correct understanding of inspiration is the following statement from *Dei Verbum*, the Vatican II document on Scripture. 'The books of Scripture, firmly, faithfully and without error, teach that truth which God, for the sake of our salvation, wished to see confided to the sacred Scriptures.' Very simply, when we state that Scripture is inspired, we are expressing the belief that God has seen to it that the Bible contains whatever truth we need for our salvation and that it cannot, rightly understood, lead us astray.

This does not mean that the Bible is correct on all matters of science or of history. It does not mean that the human authors were incapable of getting any of their facts wrong. But our salvation does not depend on accuracy in science or history or peripheral details. Our belief in inspiration (and we should remember that this is a matter of faith) is like a guarantee that God, in Scripture, gives us everything that we need. The Bible does not satisfy our curiosity, and in many respects it can be quite spartan in matters of detail. We might like, for example, to have more information regarding Jesus' earlier life, or his family background. But facts like those are not necessary for our salvation. St Paul's Second Letter to Timothy sums up the implications of inspiration as follows: 'All Scripture is inspired by God and is useful for teaching, for reproof, for correction, and for training in righteousness' (2 Tim 3:16).

Revealed

Another way in which we underline the authority of the Bible is to say that it is *revealed*, or contains *revelation*. Tabloid journalism, through the ingenuity and industry of reporters, regularly lays claims to 'startling revelations' of one kind or another. But the word revelation, as applied to the Bible, means that what we read there could not be the fruit of human effort alone. At its most literal, the word means an 'uncovering' or 'disclosure,' and the disclosure in Scripture is God's initiative. In the Scriptures, God chooses to uncover something of himself and his plans to us. He is the unknowable, hidden God (Is 45:15), whose compassion leads him to 'open up' to humanity. Perhaps more than anything else, the term 'revelation' makes the point that in his dealings with humanity, God takes the initiative. While human beings can have a certain 'natural' knowledge of God, the self-revelation of God in the Bible is far more than we could access simply through our own reflection.

A temptation which has always been present for human beings is to seek more information than we have been given in matters of faith. Fortune telling, tarot cards, the use of mediums etc. are the antithesis to biblical faith, because they try forcefully to reveal what is hidden. The fact that God, in the Scriptures, reveals himself to humanity, is an invitation to trust that he has not sold us short, but has given us all the 'information' and wisdom we need. Recourse to esoteric means in the pursuit of further 'revelation' would show an attitude of radical mistrust in God.

What the Scriptures are not

In our introduction, we noted that we would reflect not only on what prayer and the Bible *are*, but also on what they *are not*. We have done this in the case of prayer, and it is just as important that we now try to root out some misconceptions regarding Scripture.

Not history 'pure and simple'

The Bible is clearly a historical book. Much of it consists of accounts – sometimes quite detailed – of events which have occurred in the past. Yet the Bible is not history 'pure and simple'. We tend to expect written history to be a cool, detached, objective statement of events as they happened. However, any serious student of history will know that things are not quite that simple: there is no such thing as a totally detached account. It is impossible to write a history without contributing at least some 'slant' of one's own. This is the case with regard to modern history, and it is the case with regard to the history contained in the Bible. The Bible is indeed a historical book, but the history it contains has a particular 'slant': that of faith.

Let us illustrate this with a simple example. When Jesus died on Calvary, the people looking on saw a man die by crucifixion. The bare 'historical fact' was that an individual, whom some people had considered to be the Christ (the Messiah), died on a cross that day. Many – indeed most – of the witnesses saw nothing more. Later on, when the Gospels came to be written, the followers of Jesus believed that no one less than the Son of God had died on the cross that day, and that he had died in order to reconcile humanity with God. In other words, the followers of Jesus interpreted the 'bare fact' of Jesus' death in the light of their faith. One of the greatest of these early followers, St Paul, put it plainly when he wrote, 'Christ died, for our sins' (1 Cor 15:3). Even an unbeliever could accept the first part of that statement, the bare fact that Christ – or a person thought to have been the Christ – had died on Calvary. But only a believer could accept the second part, that this individual had died 'for our sins'.

In reality, the Bible is full of 'faith interpretations' of historical events. Some interpretations are subtle, some are not, but for the biblical writers, all events were marked by the presence and action of God. It simply was not the intention of the biblical writers to give the 'bare facts'. They could not do other than view events through the filter of their faith.

This does not mean that we should be sceptical about what we read in the Bible, but it reminds us that when we read the Bible, we are reading a faith account of God's actions, rather than something written by an uninvolved onlooker with a reporter's notebook. To put this in other words, the Bible was written *by* believers, *for* believers, rather than by historians for historians.

These remarks can be an important caution against biblical *fundamentalism*, which believes that wherever we find a past tense in the Bible, we have a simple, literal, historical statement of fact. This approach might seem to simplify the Bible enormously, but in fact it raises more questions than it answers. In addition, fundamentalism suggests that God is limited to just one kind of literature (history writing), and that he cannot use other forms such as story, fable, etc. to communicate the truth. The reality is that Scripture – much like the events of our lives – not only *reveals* God, it also *conceals* him. Encountering God in the pages of the Bible calls us to a more committed effort than simply opening a page and experiencing the full truth as easily as we can read.

Finally, the fact that the Bible contains a faith interpretation of the events which it recounts is a reminder and an encouragement to believers to seek a faith interpretation of the events of their own lives. The 'bare bones' of our experience are obvious to us, but our faith invites us to interpret our experience in a particular way. Putting a faith 'slant' on our lives does not mean that our version of events becomes unreliable. On the contrary, it is through our faith that we come to know the deepest truth of events.

Not simply a book of prayers and meditations

The Bible is not only inspired, it is also inspiring. Down through the centuries, some of the greatest art and literature has taken its inspiration from the pages of Scripture. Less spectacularly, though just as importantly, individual believers take inspiration for their lives from passages which speak in a special way to them. While this is just at it should be, we will also do well to remember that the Bible is far more than a collection of inspirational writings, or a resource book to be dipped into for readings to meet varying needs and moods.

The Bible is bigger than any single believer. We should be wary of approaching it with the idea that we have grasped it, or that we are doing no more than returning to old, familiar territory. Even the most well-thumbed passage in our Bible may *grasp us* in a new way, but this is more likely to happen if we try to guard against excessive familiarity. In our encounters with the Bible, we would do well to approach it as something wild and unpredictable, rather than as something domesticated.

Much of the Bible is quite obscure, and a natural reaction to this is to stick to the familiar. We each have our favourite passages – perhaps verses which we find particularly consoling and encouraging. This is, of course, a good thing, especially when we remain open to allowing passages to speak to us in a new way. In practice, most people's favourite passages are texts which are notable for their warmth, and which speak most eloquently in times of emotional need. This highlights both the value of familiarity with such passages, and the limitation of confining ourselves to our favourite texts.

There are many texts in Scripture which we may need to hear, even if we are not spontaneously drawn to them. It is highly unlikely that anyone might have as a favourite passage Matthew 5:28, where Jesus warns, 'I say to you that everyone who looks at a woman with lust has already committed adultery with her in his heart.' Equally unlikely candidates for favourite-passage status might be such challenging passages as 1 John 4:20, Jeremiah 7:1-15, or Matthew 5:21-26. We are more readily drawn to consolation than to challenge, but we need both. While it is a blessing to be familiar with passages which build up what is weak in us, this should not be at the cost of ignorance of passages which may clean away what is sinful or irrelevant. As Jesus himself tells his disciples, 'You have already been cleansed by the word that I have spoken to you' (Jn 15:3). The most tender and consoling passages may cleanse us of fear or anxiety, but we also need exposure to texts which cleanse us in less comfortable ways.

While we can and should pray with particular texts, we should also remember that the totality of a given biblical book may be far greater than the sum of its parts. Having some understanding of the *context* of a particular passage will help us to understand the passage itself, and to see how it might speak to our own context. If we wish to take the Bible seriously, we may eventually need to apply ourselves to reading and reflecting on books in their entirety, and perhaps to learning something about the background to the Bible. That is not to say that only those with the inclination to study can pray the Bible properly, but even a little extra knowledge can inject a lot of fresh life into our reading of the Bible.

Not a book of answers to life's questions

For very many people, religion is something of a 'fire service,' which they call upon in times of emergency. God himself does not examine the spiritual track-record of someone who calls out to him in a moment of need, but from a human point of view, it may be difficult to find faith sufficient for a time of crisis if there has not been a regular exercise of faith. Rather like a muscle, faith can atrophy if it is not exercised. Something similar is the case with the Bible. It can be approached as though it were a kind of emergency literature, almost like the family medical encyclopaedia, which remains on the shelf until someone feels an urgent need to consult it; but the word of God will have power only in the lives of those who turn to it regularly.

The Bible, however, is not a collection of insights, or a book of straightforward answers to life's questions. Certainly, it contains great wisdom; it abounds with practical insights which can be applied to daily living. But it does not spoon-feed us – it does not dish out pat answers to our deepest questions. It may be a very wholesome thing to 'consult' our Bible, to 'see what it says' about a specific matter, but this will not dispense with the need to trust and hope in God. As we have seen, a trustful openness to God is part of the nature of prayer. In God we indeed find the answers to our deepest questions, but these answers come slowly, perhaps maturing over an entire lifetime. They are not given to us printed on a page.

To think of the Bible as life's great 'recipe book' would be to sell it short, and to underestimate our own standing as free and intelligent creatures called into a relationship of trust with our Creator.

There is a further reason why we should resist a reading of the Bible that is driven too much by a quest for solutions to problems and answers to questions. Our questions are just that: *our* questions. Important though they may be, they are not the only questions, and perhaps not even the best questions. They may not necessarily be the questions that the Lord would have us ask. If we remain excessively focused on personal issues, we may be less able to see a bigger picture, and therefore less open to the God whose thoughts are not our thoughts, whose ways are not our ways.

Not an open book

We have already insisted that the Bible, despite its strangeness and distance from our modern culture, should not be considered a 'closed book'. It is by no means the exclusive preserve of scholars and experts in ancient languages. However, in just as real a sense, the Bible is not entirely an 'open book'. A journey through Scripture might be compared to a journey through unfamiliar territory, and for such a journey, we will benefit enormously if we have a guide. In the Acts of the Apostles, Philip the missionary meets an Ethiopian official, and hears him reading from his Bible. Acts reports the following snippet from their conversation: '"Do you understand what you are reading?" He replied, "How can I, unless someone guides me?"' (Acts 8:30-31).

Our Scripture-guide *par excellence* is the Church, which is entrusted with the task of ensuring the correct interpretation and teaching of Scripture. That is not to say that the Church has some kind of authority 'over' the Bible. Rather, the Church is in the service of the word of God, and it carries out this service by seeking to ensure that this word is correctly understood. In this regard, the Church's role might be compared to that of an interpreter working for a head of state on a foreign trip. The interpreter has a clear authority in his or her role of communicating the politician's words, but is also in the service of those words. In spite of its teaching role, however, the Church very rarely insists on specific interpretations for particular passages of Scripture. In practice, there is a great deal of freedom within the boundaries of correct interpretation.

In practice also, it is a blessing to have a guide close to hand in one's reading and praying of the Bible. This might be in the form of a good introductory book, or of a Bible study or *lectio divina* group. In prayer, as in life, remaining in contact with others helps to keep us balanced and whole.

NOTES

1. All biblical quotations are taken from the *New Revised Standard Version*.

Part Two

Introducing *Lectio Divina*

Bringing Prayer and Scripture together

We noted at the very beginning, and it follows from much of what we have seen since, that prayer and Scripture belong together: they are, or should be, inseparable. One could say that there is a relationship of interdependence between them. Prayer *needs* Scripture if it is to be authentic, a personal response to the words of a personal God. Likewise, Scripture calls for prayer just as any invitation calls for a response.

In Jesus' time, careful study of the Bible was one of the hallmarks of the devout Jew. It would hardly be exaggerated to expect this to be a hallmark of the devout Christian also. However, Jesus himself was keenly aware that study alone was no guarantee of openness to God's word. Jesus, the Word of God made flesh, experienced the sad irony of rejection by some of the greatest Scripture experts of his day: 'You search the scriptures because you think that in them you have eternal life; and it is they that testify on my behalf. Yet you refuse to come to me to have life' (Jn 5:39-40). Paradoxically, some of the very people who saw themselves as experts in the Scriptures were among those *least* likely to hear what

God was actually saying. Their knowledge, good in itself, was not accompanied by humble openness to God, and so led them to presumption rather than to true wisdom.

Jesus was not, of course, 'anti-intellectual'. He did not object to careful study of the Scriptures, but such study needed to be accompanied by an open, prayerful attitude. Human intelligence, as we have already indicated, is not sufficient to teach us the things of God. It must be accompanied by childlike trust. This is the meaning of Jesus' prayer: 'I thank you, Father, Lord of heaven and earth, because you have hidden these things from the wise and the intelligent and have revealed them to infants' (Mt 11:25). Jesus is not critical of wisdom and intelligence in themselves: these are gifts from God, to be received with gratitude and applied with diligence. Of itself, however, study will not fully open the Scriptures to us. Study is a starting-point, a means to an end. The end is prayer, relationship with God, growth in discipleship.

If Scripture calls for prayer, it is just as true that prayer is totally dependent on Scripture. Prayer, we have insisted, is fundamentally a *response* to God's initiative; a 'yes' to God's invitation. It is above all in the Bible that we encounter, in depth, the initiative and invitation of God. Implied in much of what we have said regarding prayer is that it is more about *listening* than speaking. Above all others, it is the words of Scripture that call us to listen, to hear what the Lord is saying to us.

The verb to listen, or hear, is one of the most frequently recurring in the entire Bible. It is a verb whose subject is the heart more so than the ear. It is used to call God's people not merely to detect sounds, but to let the words of God sink in, so that they can give shape to life, outlook and behaviour. The most important prayer for pious Jews – in Jesus' time and still today – is the *shema* (Hebrew for *listen!*). This is the biblical prayer which begins, 'Hear, O Israel…' (Deut 6:4; quoted by Jesus in Mk 12:29). When God's people failed to listen to his word, God raised up the prophets, giving them the task of reminding people to 'hear the word of the Lord' (Jer 2:4). The prophet Ezekiel was instructed to speak God's word to the people 'whether they hear or refuse to hear' (Ezek 2:5).

Whenever there has been a breakdown in a relationship, the key to recovery is renewed listening. Groups or individuals who are at loggerheads generally want to *tell* each other, to insist rather than to listen. It is only when people begin to listen that real communication becomes possible once again. Similarly, all renewal of God's people, within the Church, or within the life of the individual believer, requires a renewed and fresh hearing of the word of God.

The parable of the sower (Mk 4) is all about how people hear, or fail to hear, and the effects which God's word has, or fails to have, in their lives. Jesus tells us that those who hear his word and act upon it have a solid foundation for their lives, in contrast to those who hear but fail to act (Mt 7:24-27). We can never fully 'hear' the word of God. This is due to both the poverty of our nature and the richness of the word. On the one hand, God's word is inexhaustible – it carries more meaning than we can take from it at any one time. On the other hand, even when we have a good grasp of the meaning of a passage from the Bible, our human weakness can leave us unable to benefit by it. For example, Jesus' teaching on anxiety (Mt 6:25-34) is utterly simple, but it can take a lifetime of listening before it yields its fruit in the life of the believer. Our walk with God calls for constant exposure to his word: prayer calls for Scripture just as any relationship calls for listening.

The expression 'lectio divina'

Lectio divina can provide us with a clear overall framework in which to unite our prayer and our reading of Scripture. We will shortly begin to outline this framework and see how it can be put into practice, but first let us examine the term *lectio divina* itself.

As anyone who has studied a foreign language knows, some expressions simply do not translate directly from one language into another, but must be explained and interpreted. This certainly applies to the term *lectio divina*. At their most literal, these two Latin words mean 'sacred [or 'divine'] reading', but this does not at all adequately convey the full sense of the term. The word *lectio* means 'reading', and it is related to another Latin word (*lego*) which means 'collect', or 'gather'. When we read Scripture, we do so not just as an intellectual exercise, but with the intention of *gathering* its meaning and making that meaning part of our lives. This gathering is as much a matter of the heart as it is of the mind.

Clearly the word *divina* is related to the English word 'divine'. When we read Scripture, it is the divine word, the word of God, that we read. Together, the words *lectio divina* underline the twin reality of God's initiative and our response. *Lectio divina* is the process through which we encounter God's word. In this process, we progress from an *understanding* of the word to the realisation that it is God's word *to us*, a word which invites a *response*. These three phases or movements – understanding, application of the word to ourselves, and response to the word – are the heart of *lectio divina*.

Lectio divina today

We have insisted that prayer and Scripture are inseparable, but what about the generations of believers – and this applies especially to Catholics – who have lived out their Christian calling with little or no contact with the Bible? Does our insistence on the importance of Scripture not make light of their experience? And why, until quite recently, have so many Catholics grown up with the vague notion that reading the Bible is 'a Protestant thing'?

Our present insistence on the centrality of Scripture in the life of the believer does not make little of the religious experience of our grandparents' generation; nor, for that matter, does it automatically raise the quality of our own discipleship. If earlier generations lived without the Bible, they did not live without the word of God. Insofar as they lacked direct, personal contact with the word, they may have experienced some degree of spiritual malnutrition; yet the Lord does not limit his attention to those who read the Bible. An emphasis on the place of Scripture in the lives of all believers should be seen as a blessing for us, and not as a criticism of earlier generations.

In our time, we have indeed been blessed with a renewed emphasis on the Bible in the life of the Church and of the believer. One aspect of this renewal has been a rediscovery of the ancient practice of *lectio divina*. But where did this renewal come from, and why was it necessary?

One of the great, and tragic, watersheds in the history of Christianity was the sixteenth century Reformation. This was a reaction against what had become a powerful, corrupt and decadent Church. The key figure in the Reformation was Martin Luther, a biblical scholar who rejected papal authority and broke away from the Church. One of Luther's key reforming slogans was *sola scriptura*, Scripture alone. He considered Scripture to be sufficient, in itself, as an authority and guide for the individual believer. Luther rejected the claim of the Catholic Church to be the ultimate authority in the interpretation of the Bible. As a counter-reaction, the Catholic Church not only strengthened its insistence on its own role as the interpreter of Scripture, but also stressed the dangers of personal, private interpretation. Reading of the Bible by individual believers came to be viewed with suspicion, and the Council of Trent (convened to renew the Catholic Church in the wake of the Reformation) decreed that direct access to the Scriptures was not desirable for the average believer.

It has been noted that, in the wake of the Reformation, the Church was rather like a divided family, with two opposing groups each taking a share of the family silver. The reformers took the Bible, and the Catholics held on to the sacraments and devotions. This is a highly simplified picture, but it accurately reflects the fact that the Bible was, to a great extent, 'removed' from the sphere of daily Catholic life. In the centuries following the Reformation, Catholics were nourished not by direct contact with the Bible, but by 'spiritual reading,' which generally consisted of books of meditations and the lives of the saints. Such material may have helped to fill a need, but it was a weak substitute, and has accurately been described as 'crumbs from the table of the word'.

How long could such a situation last – where the people of God were being sheltered, even protected, from the word of God? Not indefinitely, and by around the middle of the twentieth century, the Church was actively encouraging all Catholics to read the Bible. This came about as a result of a range of factors, such as the enormous growth in biblical studies and the ecumenical movement. The principal Vatican II document on the subject of Scripture in the Church exhorts all the faithful to frequent reading of the Scriptures, reminding them of the words of St Jerome: 'Ignorance of the Scriptures is ignorance of Christ'.

Defining lectio divina

Lectio divina is an ancient monastic practice, the expression itself dating from the fourth century. There have been, and are, varying approaches to *lectio divina*, with different styles or shades of emphasis. We will follow one specific, clear approach to *lectio divina.* As our starting point, we will take a definition given in a recent (1993) Church document:

> *Lectio divina is a reading, on an individual or communal level, of a more or less lengthy passage of Scripture, received as the Word of God and leading, at the prompting of the Spirit, to meditation, prayer and contemplation.*

The four key elements here are *reading, meditation, prayer* and *contemplation.* The equivalent Latin words are *lectio, meditatio, oratio* and *contemplatio.* We will keep to the Latin terms, since each of the English words may already carry a certain 'baggage' of meaning, and it may be helpful to use words which, because unfamiliar, are more likely to be neutral. For the remainder of this second part of the book, we will examine these four elements in turn, and apply them to some passages from the Bible.

Lectio

In examining the process of *lectio divina*, our aim is not to theorise excessively, but to *practise* it on texts from the Bible. However, in what follows, we will spend some time reflecting on each stage of *lectio divina*, before applying it to particular biblical texts. It may be worth repeating at this stage that *lectio divina*, while providing us with a clear approach to the Scriptures, is not some kind of recipe or formula. When we pray the Scriptures with this method, we do not put on a straitjacket; rather, we give a focus and a direction to our reading of God's word.

It is self-evident that the first approach to any

text is simply to read it. However, although we generally take the act of reading for granted, there is much about it that is less than self-evident. If we pick up a specialist text, for example one dealing with engineering or economics, we will not, unless we have the necessary education, expect to understand it fully. If we read an introduction to one of those subjects, we can realistically expect to understand more of what we read than in the first case. When we read, therefore, we automatically modify our approach and our expectations, according to the type of material we are reading. When reading the daily paper, we bring a different mindset to the letters page than to the day's leading article, and it would be a very poor investor who approached the shares listings with the same expectation that he or she brought to the weather forecast.

In practice, however, many people read the Bible with a directness and even a naïveté that they would not bring to other reading material. This does not do justice to the Bible as the word of God. It is not that we should think of God's word as being necessarily obscure or complicated, but by bringing all our powers of discernment and understanding to bear on it, we simply do it justice as the utterly important material it is.

When we read, we do so in order to *understand*. Like much else of what we read, the word of God often requires explanation before it can be understood. In the Bible itself there are texts which make this abundantly clear. The author of the Second Letter of Peter is concerned that the community to which he is writing will not be lead astray by some of the more obscure points in Paul's letters.

'There are some things in them,' he writes, 'hard to understand, which the ignorant and unstable twist to their own destruction' (2 Pet 3:16). This New Testament writer was certainly not attempting to put people off reading the Scriptures (although we might note that he was writing before Paul's letters were officially considered to be a part of the Bible). Instead, he was concerned that their reading be intelligent and well-informed. He was aware that those whose reading is poorly informed may not only fail to benefit from such reading, but risk falling into serious error.

In Luke's Gospel (24:27 and context), we have a lovely example of how Jesus himself explains the meaning of the Scriptures to his disciples. This text is a particularly important one for those who wish to pray the Scriptures. It underlines the importance of communication with the Lord if we are to understand his word fully. In this chapter of Luke's Gospel, two disciples of Jesus are leaving Jerusalem, just after the passion and death of Jesus. They are crushed by the events of recent days; their hope has been dashed by the death of the Master, an event beyond which they are unable to see.

The journey of these two disciples away from Jerusalem can symbolise the turning away of anyone whose life's experience crushes their faith and leaves them unable to believe that a loving God holds all of reality in his hands. What changed the outlook of these two broken disciples was a fresh encounter with the risen Lord himself. Jesus himself showed them the meaning of passages in the Scriptures which were beyond their intelligence. He showed them the inevitability of suffering, and pointed out the passages in the Bible which had predicted that he himself would suffer and die.

Very often, the 'intelligence' or wisdom of the Bible not only surpasses human understanding, but runs counter to it. It is precisely where God's intelligence is far beyond ours, where 'God's foolishness is wiser than human wisdom' (1 Cor 1:25) that we most need the assistance of the Spirit of God in our efforts to understand and pray the Bible. From the moment we open our Bible, we will do well to pray for the help and guidance of the Holy Spirit.

Of course, it is not only on a 'spiritual' level that our intelligence needs assistance. Since the Bible is the word of God in human words, we must also apply ourselves to the fullest possible reading of the Bible as human literature. For decades, biblical scholarship has taken full advantage of the best insights of the study of secular literature, and even if we neither wish nor need to go into such matters in detail, this does remind us that the Bible is to be taken seriously as human literature.

The term 'biblical criticism' is often used to describe the whole scholarly effort to understand the Bible as well and as profoundly as possible. This might sound like a rather negative approach to the word of God, and one might be inclined to ask who is qualified to criticise God's word. However, biblical criticism is generally carried out by those who are passionate about the Bible (in much the same way that art critics are passionate about art). In biblical criticism, in fact, the object of criticism is not so much the Bible itself, as the way in which we read the Bible. Biblical criticism questions much of what readers might be inclined to take for granted, and reminds us that the Scriptures demand respect and effort. For this reason, those who wish to pray the Bible may benefit greatly by some contact – however small – with the fruits of biblical criticism or scholarship.

Here we might stress once again that the Bible is not the exclusive preserve of scholars: it is God's word to all of his people. But our reading of Scripture can really come to life if it is supported by a little background knowledge. We will see this when we begin to practise *lectio divina* on a few passages from the Bible.

Let us anticipate an objection which might be raised at this point: 'I want to pray the Bible, and grow in my relationship with God. I want nourishment, not dry head-knowledge!' This is, to some extent, an understandable reaction, but it is based on a wrong expectation. It would make as much sense to complain: 'I want to play the piano, to make beautiful music. I don't want to play boring scales!' The efforts which we make to grasp the meaning of the Bible are not unlike practising the scales in order to play the piano. *Lectio*, reading, is the first step in praying the Bible, and we read in order to understand. It follows that any effort on our part to deepen our understanding of what we read can be seen as an aspect of our prayer. In the strictest sense, background study is not *lectio divina*: we do not practise *lectio divina* on a guide to the Bible, or on a biblical commentary. However, our reading of this kind of material can be taken up into our *lectio divina*. Scripture study becomes a prayer when its final aim is living in accordance with God's word.

Depending on the type of biblical text we are

reading, an important part of careful *lectio* may be to guard against, or even to break down, any over-familiarity with the text. Much of what we read will reflect a mentality, a world-view and a culture which is distant from our own. We do well not to presume that we have understood a passage or a story simply because we can read it. We may need to be prepared to leave our own world, if we are to enter into the world of the Bible. Our hospitality towards the word of God will include a concern on our part to receive it as it is, with openness, rather than inadvertently stamping it with our own prejudices or expectations.

In *lectio*, the initial stage of *lectio divina*, our fundamental concern is with the passage we are reading *in itself*. We are not yet reflecting on the passage, or trying to apply it to our lives. Rather, what we are doing at this time is trying to become fully acquainted with the passage, as a preparation for the reflection which will follow at the *meditatio* stage. In *lectio*, our concern is to grasp the *meaning* of what we are reading. This is not to say that every passage in the Bible is limited to a single meaning only. The same passage may speak differently to different individuals, depending on their circum-stances and needs. However, our reflection on the Scriptures needs to be guided by what the biblical authors intended when they wrote, that is, the meaning of the passage in itself.

While many biblical texts may have a much fuller meaning for us today than they did for their writers, our reflection on them needs to be anchored in and guided by their 'original' meaning and context. Otherwise, we risk using the Bible as a springboard for the meanderings of our imagination. A little background knowledge not only opens up the world of the Bible to us – it can help to keep our prayerful reflection properly grounded in the Bible itself. This will become particularly clear when we reflect on a passage from the book of the Apocalypse.

When we are doing *lectio divina*, it is best – especially when we are beginning – to focus on a single, self-contained passage (for example an episode from one of the Gospels; or a Psalm). It may help to underline words or phrases that strike us (although some people prefer not to mark their Bible in any way), or to look up related passages referred to in the margin of our Bible. The context of the passage (what precedes and follows it) will often help us to appreciate it better. Depending on the type of passage, we might focus on the characters involved, their situation and concerns, and how they relate to each other. If we are particularly taken with a passage, it may also be well worth the effort to learn it by heart. In fact, the latter is a very revealing experience: when we commit words to memory, they are then in a good position to touch our heart! Taking the trouble to learn some of the words of Scripture by heart is also a clear statement on our part that we are taking the Lord's words seriously. Anthony of Egypt, one of the great saints of the early Church, was reputed to have known the entire Bible by heart!

Let us now begin some practical exercises in *lectio*! We will take three passages (Gen 12:1-4; Lk 15:11-32; Rev 13:1-18), and examine each of them in turn. We will do so again after we have introduced *meditatio* and *oratio*.

Genesis 12:1-4

At this point, take a few moments to read Genesis 12:1-4. This short passage describes God's call of Abraham, his promise of great blessings, and Abraham's obedient response. Having read it, we could immediately begin to reflect on God's call of each of his children, and on how trusting obedience brings us great blessings. However, a more careful reading will reveal a striking depth of meaning in these few lines from the first book of the Bible.

For a really full understanding of the call of Abraham, we need to go right back to the beginning of the book of Genesis, to the opening verses of the Bible. There we read that God created the whole of reality, and that his whole creation was good. The highpoint of creation was man and woman, made in God's very image (Gen 1:27). Sadly, this story of original blessing comes to a rapid end. In the third chapter of the Bible, we read how man and woman are tempted into mistrust of God; into doubting his love and care for them (Gen 3:1-5). Their lack of trust leads to rebellion and disobedience, with disastrous consequences.

We are used to thinking of the story of Genesis 3 as 'the fall,' the description of how the first man and woman fell from their position of blessedness and harmony with God. This is quite correct, but in fact the fall only *begins* here. The next several chapters of Genesis detail the continuing fall of humanity, presenting a steadily worsening situation. From a simple act disobedience, there is a rapid progression to fratricide (Gen 4:8) and even the threat of mass-murder (Gen 4:23-24). In chapter 6, God resolves to begin anew, wiping out everyone but the faithful Noah and his family.

After the great flood, the descendants of Noah multiply and spread throughout the world. This is in obedience to the original command to be fruitful and multiply (Gen 1:28), which God renewed immediately following the flood (Gen 9:1). It now appears that a real recovery is underway within humanity. But this is not to last. People became uneasy at the prospect of being 'scattered abroad upon the face of the whole earth' (Gen 11:4), and instead of trusting in God, grasp at the false security of a city, and a tower which would reach to the heavens. God's reaction to this act of disobedience is to bring about just what people had tried to avoid: they will now indeed be scattered throughout the earth, and instead of the false, self-sufficient security they had sought by banding together, they find themselves unable to communicate with each other.

What is God to do with this truculent humanity, incapable of sustained obedience? At this point, we witness what appears to be a change of tactics on God's part. He seems to give up on the idea of converting humanity *en masse*, but opts to work with a single individual, through whose obedience he plans to bless everyone else. This individual is Abraham, a descendant of one of those who had been scattered across the face of the earth.

Why Abraham? The Bible does not give a reason, and we are to understand that this is simply God's free, sovereign choice. Abraham's obedience is unquestioning: note the perfect correspondence in the passage, between v. 1, 'the Lord said to Abraham,' and v. 4, 'So Abraham went.' God's choice, along with Abraham's obedient response, gives rise to a new beginning, which will eventually lead to the blessing of all humanity (v. 3). Little wonder, then, that pious Jews considered themselves to be the 'descendants of Abraham' (Jn 8:33). Throughout the Bible, Abraham is considered to the 'hero' of faith. In the New Testament, he is mentioned no less than 73 times!

The pattern of God's call and Abraham's obedient response is often repeated, and it becomes the model for Christian discipleship. We can see this pattern clearly in Mary's 'yes' to God's invitation to her to play a special role in his plans (Lk 1:38). In the call of the first disciples (Mk 1:16-18), there is a clear reflection of Abraham's reaction to God's call: 'Jesus said to them, "follow me,"… and immediately they left their nets and followed him.'

By now, it is clear that the call of Abraham in Genesis 12:1-4 is much more than the call of an isolated individual to faith and trust in God. It is the story of how obedience can alter the course of history! This became clear through an examination of the biblical context of the passage, and with this background, our meditation on the passage will be far richer than it could possibly be if were to take the passage on its own, detached from its broader context.

Luke 15:11-32

There is hardly a better-known story in the entire Bible than the parable of the prodigal son (Lk 15:11-32). This story, familiar to believers and unbelievers alike, is generally considered to be the greatest of the parables of Jesus. However, our familiarity with the passage can breed, if not contempt, at least a certain immunity to its message. When we hear the opening words, 'There was a man who had two sons,' there may be a tendency – or a temptation – to think, 'I've heard this before!' Our listening (and this applies also to our reading) then becomes superficial, since we don't expect to hear anything new.

The best way to 'rehabilitate' the story is to situate it squarely in its biblical context. This marvellous passage from Luke's Gospel is, if anything, a victim of the title which is generally given to it: 'the parable of the prodigal son.' In fact there are three main characters in the story, not just one. They are all introduced in the opening words, which we have quoted above. The story of the prodigal son is but one part of the full story. If we read the parable with only him in mind, we will read a beautiful story of an errant son, now contrite, returning to a loving, forgiving parent. Meditating on it, we might focus on our own need for repentance, or on the times when we have experienced God's forgiveness. This would already be a wonderfully rich meditation, but the full riches of the parable are greater still.

The parable is actually the last of three parables Jesus told in response to a complaint made about him by the scribes and Pharisees: 'This fellow welcomes sinners and eats with them' (Lk 15:2. The same complaint is made in Lk 5:30 and 19:7). From a human point of view, this complaint was not unreasonable. The scribes and Pharisees were very religious people, concerned to observe the law of God to the last detail. Since God was a God of infinite holiness, they believed that strict avoidance of all that was unholy was required of all those whom he had called. This included the complete avoidance of sinners – those who, by definition, were unholy. Little wonder that they took offence at the behaviour of Jesus, who not only mixed with sinners, but claimed to be doing so in the name of God! Jesus' behaviour (and his justification of it: 'The Son of Man came to seek out and to save the lost,' Lk 19:10) called into question the scribes' and Pharisees' conviction that they were in a special, exclusive relationship with God. They who served God so faithfully resented the idea that God did not confine his love to them, but extended it in equal measure to outcasts and sinners.

It was to these upright, conscientious, religious people that Jesus addressed the parable of the prodigal son. It was not addressed – at least not in its original setting – to obvious sinners, even though this is how it tends to be read and heard by most people today. The figure of the older brother in the parable, resentful of his father's prodigal generosity towards his younger brother, will have resonated clearly, and uncomfortably, with Jesus' original audience. Following, as it does, on the parables of the lost sheep and the lost coin, the parable of the prodigal son suggests that the righteous elder brother is every bit as lost as his younger brother. While the younger son was lost away from home, his older sibling was lost in his father's house, just as the sheep was lost away in the wilderness, while the coin was lost at home.[1]

Jesus is hinting (and not all that subtly) that some of the most scrupulously religious people of his day may be just as 'lost' as the sinners whom they despise.

Like the older son who remained at home, the Pharisees remained strictly within the covenant. Like the older son, who could not fathom his father's love for his sinful brother, they refused to accept the fact that God could be so generous with his love. While obvious sinners will have heard the parable gladly, as an invitation to turn to God and trust in his love, it contained a more challenging message for the scribes and Pharisees. In essence, the parable of the prodigal son told the scribes and Pharisees that they had it all wrong: God is not an exclusive God, waiting to condemn sinners and those who live outside of the covenant. He is a loving Father, who rejoices in the repentant sinner, whether or not the sinner is a member of his covenant people. In Jesus, God's promise to Israel through the prophet Zephaniah, 'He will rejoice over you with gladness, he will renew you in his love' (Zeph 3:17), has been extended to everyone. Those who could not accept God's generosity ran the risk of a self-imposed exclusion from the celebration, just like the older brother in the parable.

An exclusive focus on the older brother does no more justice to the parable than a similarly exclusive focus on his younger sibling. The two must be kept together, and both must be related to the person of the father, who loves his two children equally. Here, we have concentrated on the older brother, but only in order to show that this parable is not just about the prodigal son. Honest reflection on the fact that religious people stand just as much in need of repentance as do notorious sinners, and that they are likely to be closer in temperament to the dutiful older brother than to his wayward sibling, will add salt to our meditation on this extraordinarily rich parable.

Revelation 13

The book of Revelation (or the Apocalypse) is the most dramatic – and the most dramatically misunderstood – book in the entire Bible. As a book, Revelation tends to evoke either of two quite opposite responses. One is to dismiss the whole book as bizarre nonsense; the other is to read it as a literal prediction of events which will accompany the end of the world. The thirteenth chapter of Revelation, the text for our third *lectio*, is the most dramatic and misunderstood part of the book. Without some knowledge of the background to the book, this chapter is utterly unintelligible. On the other hand, with even a brief explanation, it can be seen to be an exceptionally inspiring text.

Take a few moments to read through Revelation 13, and allow yourself to be struck by the grotesque intensity of the imagery. Who or what do these fearsome creatures represent? How could one possibly *pray* such a text? Perhaps the first thing to note is that there is nothing in the text that demands that we take the images *literally*. They are to be interpreted, rather than viewed as photographic reproductions of reality. The warning at the end of the chapter, 'This calls for wisdom' (v. 18) could be applied not just to the riddle of the number 666, but to the whole chapter. A rush to label the beasts is foolish, and will lead to foolish conclusions. Wise interpretation will tread more slowly, and yield more wholesome insights.

The first step in the interpretation of Revelation 13 (and of the book as a whole) is to understand that it is an example of a very specific type of literature, known as apocalyptic. Two features of apocalyptic literature are of particular importance for our *lectio* of this chapter. Firstly, the writers of Revelation were concerned with what they perceived to be a cosmic struggle between good and evil. The victory of good over evil was assured, but the struggle unfolded in spectacular and violent fashion. Second, this type of writing uses a great deal of symbolic imagery, most notably symbolic animals and numbers. Once again, such symbols call for interpretation, rather than a naïve, literal reading.

A further item of information with which we need to be armed as we approach Revelation 13 is the readership or audience to which the book was addressed. Revelation was written for Christians either enduring, or undergoing the threat of, persecution for their Christian faith. That is to say, it was written for people who felt fundamentally at odds with, and threatened by, the world around them (or, if they did not, part of the task of Revelation was to show them the threats which their environment posed to their faith).

Turning to some of the details of Revelation 13, we can note that there are three main players in the passage: there is the dragon (v.2; also 12:7ff.), which represents Satan; there is the first beast (vv. 1-10), who is given power by the dragon; and there is the second beast (vv. 11-18), who is the delegate of the first beast. Together, these three creatures represent a kind of unholy trinity, aping the divine Trinity and deceiving those who serve the true God. A key concern of the passage is that God's faithful are being coerced into worshipping an image of the first beast, who is identified at the end of the chapter as a human being whose number is 666.

At the time Revelation was written, a particularly insidious political tool of the Roman empire was emperor worship. This was not so much a religious matter, as a way of promoting allegiance to the emperor. In various parts of the empire, local representatives of the emperor had the task of ensuring that people professed the emperor to be lord and god. In the earliest decades of Christianity, Christians were not subject to this requirement, as they were still considered to be a Jewish sect. Jews, given the strict monotheism for which they were noted, were exempt from the obligation to profess the emperor as god. However, within a few decades, Christians were viewed as fully distinct from Judaism, and therefore subject to the obligation of emperor worship just like all other non-Jews.

If one Christian – such as the writer of Revelation – wished to write to a group of other Christians, to warn them against yielding to pressure to worship the emperor, he would hardly risk exposing himself by writing his thoughts directly. It would be much safer to use a set, symbolic type of communication which he knew his audience would understand. This is what we have in Revelation 13. The author is expressing, in cryptic, encoded language, the view that emperor worship is utterly evil, from Satan (the dragon) himself, rather than a harmless expression of civic loyalty. The beast from the sea, whose image is to be worshipped, under pain of death, is the Roman emperor. The writer probably has in mind the emperor Nero, the letters of whose name add up to 666, in a simple alphabetic code which was well known at the time. Although the code was simple, it could be deciphered only by those who already knew what letters a number stood for, as many different combinations of letters could add up to a given number. The second beast, from the earth, is the local representative of the emperor, who has the power to kill anyone who will not worship the image of the first beast (v. 15). The latter is probably a reference to statues of the emperor, before which people were forced to worship.

To many people, making the appropriate noises before a statue of the Roman emperor once a year may have seemed like a harmless game of 'pretend'. But the writer of Revelation does not see it this way. Even if 'the whole earth followed the beast' (v. 3), and it 'deceives the inhabitants of the earth' (v. 14), the writer will take a stand. He is convinced that the worship of anyone other than God is inspired by Satan himself. The elevation of any human power to the status of God is so radically perverse that it can be brought about only by the great liar himself.

Those who follow God, rather than the beast, will suffer. Rome is mighty, recovering even after a period of political instability (v. 3). She will not tolerate dissent, but deal with it very brutally. The might of God is of a different kind: it is the strength of the lamb, who has conquered evil by suffering its assaults without striking back. Throughout the book, the principal image for Christ is the lamb. The second beast manages to ape the gentleness of Christ: it can appear like the lamb, v. 11. But it speaks the words of the dragon, thus revealing itself to be a ravenous wolf in sheep's clothing, the kind of deceitful figure that Jesus had warned of (Mt 7:15).

Revelation 13 sets out to strengthen believers who are experiencing the terrible paradox that the God of infinite power will not crush evil directly. He will not save his faithful from suffering, but will lead them safely through it. They are asked neither to compromise with false religion nor to resort to violent resistance against it (v. 10). They must also endure the economic hardship which will result from their loyalty to the faith (v. 17).

This passage does not in any way pull its punches, but acknowledges, in verses 7 and 15, the inevitability of defeat and death for many who remain faithful. What does it take for a believer to persevere in hope through persecution, defeat and death? Where does the strength for this attitude come from? Perseverance is possible only for those who are convinced that God is in control, and Revelation 13 leaves no doubt whatever that he is! Read through the passage again, and count the number of times the words 'was allowed' occur (or a close equivalent, depending on the translation you are using). They occur no less than four times, along with two occurrences of the phrase 'was given'. We are meant to understand that whatever the beasts do is *allowed*, whatever powers they have are *given*, by God himself.

This is the key to perseverance: the conviction that even the greatest evil is permitted by God as a part of his mysterious and infinitely wise plan. Nothing that the dragon or his agents do, no atrocity or havoc they may wreak, lies beyond God's providence. His wisdom is able to weave a pattern of salvation from even the bloodiest of threads. This is why Revelation is such a hopeful book. It candidly faces up to the greatest evil, and insists that the victory is God's.

It will be clear by now that, far from being a bizarre text, written by an unhinged author, Revelation 13 is full of Christian hope and confidence. There is perhaps no better advertisement in the Bible for the importance of good, well-informed *lectio*. Rather than dismissing this chapter as hopelessly bizarre, or using it to indulge in religious fantasy, we are now in a position to meditate fruitfully on its message.

Meditatio

In the course of our reading of these three passages, we took advantage of a certain knowledge of context and background, and of a degree of familiarity with the Bible as a whole. However, it would be unfortunate if this were taken to imply that *lectio divina* can be done only by those who have access to such knowledge. Our *lectio* has shown the value of a degree of background knowledge, and this will, hopefully, now inform our *meditatio*, but that is not to say that the whole process is limited to fully-fledged students of the Bible. While some parts of the Bible (such as certain passages from the book of Revelation) may remain practically 'closed' to those who have no background knowledge, much of the Bible can be read, reflected upon and prayed by those who have little or no such knowledge. While even the 'easiest' parts of the Bible may yield greater fruit for meditation if they are studied in some depth, they will nevertheless yield a great deal even without serious background study.

Now that we are taking the next step in the process of *lectio divina*, let us recall something we noted earlier. *Lectio divina* is not intended to be a kind of straitjacket, dictating the details of how we pray. We are presenting it in a step-by-step manner, but any given period of prayer with the Bible may not be quite so ordered. In practice, we will often be doing *meditatio*, reflecting on a passage, even as we read it. At times, the first contact with a verse of Scripture will lead us straight into prayer. Again, there may be the odd occasion when, no sooner have we opened our Bible, than we feel moved to sit quietly in contemplation. When there is an effortless, inner movement in our time of prayer with the Bible, we should follow it, rather than anxiously trying to conform to a rigid, step-by-step pattern. It might be helpful to consider the different steps in *lectio divina* as components, rather than strictly as steps which must necessarily follow each other. Without a doubt, the 'normal' route we follow will be a progression – or a struggle to progress – through the steps of *lectio divina*, but they are given to guide us, rather than to bind us.

Our *lectio* on the passages above has shown the enormous importance of *context* for the under-standing of a biblical text. It is sometimes suggested that the meaning of biblical passages is so condition-ed by their original context that they have little if any relevance for us today. In practice, however, this suggestion tends to be made regarding passages whose meaning for us today might be one with which we would rather not be confronted. A central conviction of our Christian faith is that the word of God still speaks to us, today, if we are open to hearing it. After we have tried to understand what it meant in its original context, the next stage in allowing the word to speak to us is to reflect on it, and this is the task of *meditatio*.

The transition from *lectio* to *meditatio* can be expressed in various ways: it is the movement from facts to truth; from information to insight; from knowledge to wisdom; from the biblical context to our context. Good *lectio* will give us facts, information and knowledge, but on their own, all of these are quite useless if they do not gradually lead towards *transformation*. The word of God is the word of life, not just the word of knowledge. If we read it without letting it touch our lives, we will be like the foolish man who built his house on sand. If we read it with a view to transformation and growth in discipleship, it will provide a solid foundation for our lives (Mt 7:24-27).

In *lectio*, we struggle to master the word, but we do this only so that the word might master us; we read it so that it might read us. The letter to the Hebrews makes it clear that the word of God reads the reader, where it says, 'It is able to judge the thoughts and intentions of the heart' (Heb 4:12). *Meditatio* is allowing our lives, our situations, to be read by the word which we have read. In *meditatio*, we look for points of contact between the plan of God as it unfolds in the Bible and our lives as they unfold. Conversely, *meditatio* can show us points of non-contact, obstacles and resistances to the plan of

God in our lives. The word which lights up the way also lights up the cobwebs. The word which consoles also convicts.

How do we make the transition from *lectio* to *meditatio*? Up till now, the word has been the *object* of our investigation. It has been, so to speak, 'out there,' at arm's length. Now it is time to enter into the text, to become a protagonist, an actor, a subject. Having grasped the original situation of the word in *lectio*, we are ready to see how it speaks to *our* situation.

Whereas in *lectio*, we look on or listen in as God speaks to his people, in *meditatio*, the communication becomes fully personal: it is no longer a case of God speaking to him or her, but *you* speaking to *me*. The change from *lectio* to *meditatio* is substantially a change of grammatical person, a change from 'he' and 'they' to 'you' and 'I'. When we meditate on Gospel passages, for example, we no longer listen to Jesus speaking to Mary or to the rich young man, but hear him speaking directly to us. The beatitudes (Mt 5:2-12) are no longer being spoken to a remote multitude, but are a promise and challenge to us, here and now. The exodus is no longer a distant event, shrouded in the mists of time, but God's saving intervention in our lives, today. This aspect of *meditatio*, hearing God address us personally, anticipates the next stage in *lectio divina*, in which we will address God personally.

Where the Bible contains the history of salvation, then our meditation on it tries to discover how and where this history continues to unfold in our personal (and social, family, community) history. Where the Bible records the struggle of God's people

79

to be faithful to their covenant relationship with him, *meditatio* draws in our present-day struggles to be faithful to our Christian calling. Where the Bible recounts failure and forgiveness, *meditatio* encourages us, today, to persevere in our efforts at discipleship. In order to make such connections, we need to use a little imagination. This does not mean letting our imagination run wild, or indulging in fantasy. The *lectio* which we have done will guide us, and keep our imagination on track.

In practice, the time we give to *meditatio* on a given passage may be spent reading it very slowly, chewing it over, repeating certain words or phrases. Repetition has a particularly important part to play in meditation on the word. In the monastic tradition, the image of *ruminatio*, or chewing on the word like a cow chewing the cud, was commonly used. By recalling and 'mulling over' an incident or a short text from Scripture, we reinforce within ourselves the thought and memory of the workings of God. It is not such a long step from this to a greater awareness of his workings in the details of our lives.

A further aspect of *meditatio* may be using other – related – texts to shed light on the passage with which we are praying. It may happen occasionally, while we are reflecting on a passage of Scripture, that a verse or passage from an entirely different context comes to mind. This may help to distil the message of the passage on which we are reflecting. As we grow in familiarity with the Bible, we come increasingly to realise that, in spite of its great diversity, it can also be seen as a single whole. Any given text may be illuminated by several other texts.

While doing *meditatio*, we might also ask what

values and attitudes, what judgements, what ways of looking at the world, are present in the text. In order to 'apply' a biblical text to our own situation, we need to enter into the world and values of the text.

As we continue on our itinerary through the four stages of *lectio divina* (*lectio*, *meditatio*, *oratio*, *contemplatio*), we will notice that each stage is more personal and intimate in nature than the one that precedes it. *Lectio*, of its nature, is the most 'objective'. As we have seen, this stage does not yet call for personal involvement with the text we are reading. It is possible, while doing *lectio divina*, to follow another person's *lectio*, and then continue on to the other stages. It is no longer quite the same with *meditatio*. Nobody else can fully do our *meditatio* for us. It is something that requires personal effort on our part. However, it is possible for a leader or guide at least to help with *meditatio*, and offer suggestions as to how it might be approached. With the next stage, *oratio*, or prayer, it is a different story. Nobody else can pray for us. We either pray ourselves, or not at all. We simply cannot 'piggyback' on someone else's prayer. However, even here, someone can at least share their own prayers with us, and we might eventually make those prayers our own. The fourth stage, *contemplatio*, is different still. We cannot even do *contemplatio* for ourselves, let alone pick up on someone else's efforts. This is because, as we shall see, *contemplatio* is God's gift to us, his communication of himself to us now, without the mediation of Scripture.

After our initial examination of *lectio*, we did a practical 'exercise' on three passages from the Bible. We will do the same after both *meditatio* and *oratio*.

There are no 'practical exercises' in *contemplatio*, and the reason for this will become clear in due course. For now, let us continue with some exercises in *meditatio*. Note that what we present here is not the 'doing' of *meditatio*, but the end results of one individual's reflection on the three texts. Others may be able to make these end results their own, but strictly speaking, each person needs to do his or her own reflection, if the text is to speak to him or her in a personal way. What follows should be seen merely as a guide to personal meditation, and an illustration of how one might progress from the first stage of *lectio divina* to the second.

Genesis 12:1-4

The story of the call of Abraham is a story of God's initiative. The God who called creation into existence is the one who calls people into relationship with him. Each of us has been called, and is invited to make our life a response to this call. The rest of creation will never fail to live up to its potential: light will always and only be light; animals will eat, defend themselves, reproduce. But for the human person, the highpoint of creation, God's call comes as a choice: we have the freedom to respond or to refuse.

The realisation that God makes a claim on us does away with any false notion we may have of complete autonomy. We depend on God for our very existence, and so it's hardly surprising that we should depend on him for continued well-being and happiness. Once he felt the call of God, Abraham allowed his whole life to be taken up with it. What about us? Generally speaking, we assign to God a particular part of our life: a slot, a time, an activity. While this may seem fine in practice, we need also to remember that our whole life is dependant on God. It is in him that 'we live and move and have our being' (Acts 17:28). There is great peace to be gained from the conviction that the Creator of all, the Almighty, is interested in us, calls us. How much anxiety might we spare ourselves if we could internalise this faith conviction – if we could let it sink the long, long distance from our heads to our hearts?

As felt-knowledge (rather than simple head-knowledge) this comes slowly, over the course of a lifetime, through struggles to believe, trust and remain faithful. Our growth in trust is a long journey, like the journey of Abraham. In fact, the need for trust is built into the call itself. This is because God never overwhelms our intellect with total clarity. He does not sweep us along with a certainty which cannot be resisted. There is always room for doubt, and there is always room for trust. Doubt and trust are not opposites; they are not mutually exclusive. If there were no doubt, there would be no need for trust. As the one who took his first steps with neither certainty nor security, Abraham is our model for trusting faith. He lived by trust alone.

It is not easy for us to live by trust alone. One day, we offer God our trust; the next day, anxiety reasserts itself, and we snatch back our trust. One day, we have a wonderful sense of God's providence; the next, we hear an inner voice asking, just like the serpent asked Eve, 'Did God *really* say this to you? Is he to be trusted?' We should not think that God is offended by our difficulties with trust. He is big enough to deal with them! We need to feel reassured that with God there are no 'second chances' – there is no need for them, since God does not count! Every time we start again in sincerity, renewing our trust and our commitment, we are beginning anew.

In Abraham, we can see clearly the *effects of trust*. In response to God's call, he let go of his autonomy, of his own plans and projects. Through his radical trust in God, he became a figure of hope for all of humanity, one through whom countless others would be blessed. All those who try to live lives of trust in God send out ripples to the rest of humanity: to their spouses and families; to their friends, workmates and communities. When God truly makes a difference to our lives, then our lives truly make a difference. We may not work wonders; we may not feel any different, but the Lord himself can do a great deal with our 'yes' to his will.

We might say that Abraham's obedience made him a part of the solution rather than a part of the problem. He stood apart from the rest of humanity, and helped stem the tide of wickedness and suffering that resulted from sin. Whereas mistrust and disobedience had brought great suffering – indeed a curse (cf. Gen 3:14-17), Abraham's attitude began a whole series of blessings. In him, we see an anticipation of Jesus, who prayed to the Father, 'For their sakes I sanctify myself, so that they also may be sanctified in truth' (Jn 17:19). We should never underestimate the difference we can make to others, by taking a stand for and with God.

When we read the call of Abraham, we may be struck by the fact that God is the one who does all the work! It is he who speaks, who blesses, who promises, who shows the way, who makes great. Abraham simply takes God at his word. We might therefore be inclined to think of Abraham as a silent, passive type. He might be taken as a confirmation of the suspicion many people have regarding faith: that it is for the weak. It is interesting to contrast Abraham with some of the characters in the preceding chapter. There we read about the high achievers, the architects of a city and tower. In spite of their human ingenuity, their efforts came to naught, because they were not rooted in obedience to God. On the contrary, they were working in opposition to God's plan for humanity, and so their efforts led to disunity and disruption.

The reversal of this disunity began in Abraham, the one in whom 'all the families of the earth shall be blessed' (Gen 12:3). His inner strength achieved far more than all the strenuous efforts of the builders. He teaches us that faith and obedience *call* for strength, and are in turn a *source* of strength. In the lives of many individuals, the single greatest achievement is 'letting go and letting God.' The moment they entrust themselves to God becomes, for them, the equivalent of Abraham's response to God's call: the moment of the great reversal. When a person learns to do this (whether suddenly, or over a long period of time), they experience the liberating wisdom of Psalm 127: 'Unless the Lord builds the house, those who build it labour in vain' (v. 1), and of St Paul's words to his friends at Philippi, 'I can do all things through him who strengthens me' (Phil 4:13).

Luke 15:11-32

As we suggested in our *lectio* on the parable of the prodigal son, a fruitful approach to this parable might be to shift the focus of our attention from the prodigal son to his elder brother. While we can all identify readily with the obvious sinner, we may not feel quite so comfortable with having our self-righteousness exposed. We are conditioned – quite rightly – to think of sin as turning away from God, and repentance as returning to him. It's hardly surprising, then, if we see a clear reflection of ourselves in the drama of the prodigal son. However, our religious upbringing may also have told us that the opposite to sin is careful observance and duty. Insofar as we identify with the older brother, it may be to sympathise with him: the one who has done his duty all these years does not appear to be getting the credit due to him.

Reflection on the older brother in this story may invite us to ask some very fundamental questions: 'What is my religion about?' 'What motivates my religious practice and moral behaviour?' Implicit in the older brother's remarks to his father is the complaint: 'Why should I bother to serve you so faithfully, when those who are less faithful suffer no disadvantage?' The older brother's attitude shows that he thought of his father's love as something that had to be *earned*. If this was the case, it was fundamentally unjust that his younger brother should experience the same love without having earned it. On the other hand, if even after a period of bohemian living, his brother was still loved by the father, why should he, the dutiful one, strive to please his father?

What about us? Are we trying to please the Father? To keep him happy and appease his anger? Are our efforts to live a moral life intended to help us work our way into God's good books? To the extent that this may be so, our motivation is wrong. The only worthwhile motivation – and the most effective one – for living a good Christian life is *gratitude* for the love of God. If we could earn God's love, then it would not be love. If we are convinced of God's love, then we need no other motivation. For all too many Christians, the starting point for Christian morality is the concern to avoid punishment, or at best, to win God's favour. The moral life should instead be the grateful life, the lived response to God's love.

Of course, the elder son's diligence is, in itself, commendable. He *did* serve his father better than his younger sibling. But somewhere along the line, a note of drudgery and resentment has crept into his relationship with his father. In spite of all his dedicated service, he does not really *know* his father. We too can throw ourselves into the work of the Lord to the extent that we lose contact with the Lord of the work. We can be like Martha, complaining that we are doing all the work, while the invitation simply to be with the Lord is constantly open to us (cf. Lk 10:38-42). We may need to spend a long time with the words, 'You are always with me, and all that is mine is yours.' In order to do this, we need to leave our busyness aside from time to time, and allow the Father to minister to us. It is in the Father's company that we can leave aside the question, 'what is in it for me?' The Father himself is the answer.

In the parable, the elder brother's resentment is directed specifically against the father's unconditional, 'easy' forgiveness of his wayward brother. He is like the prophet Jonah, who sulked when God forgave the inhabitants of Nineveh (Jon 3:10-4:1). However, the older brother might prompt us to reflect on the presence of resentment in any area of our lives. If we find that we are acutely aware of the sins of others, then we ourselves may be in need of healing. St Paul reminds us that love 'is not irritable or resentful,' and that it 'does not rejoice in wrongdoing' (1 Cor 13:5-6). It was the elder brother's resentment that excluded him from the celebration, and we might learn from him that resentment is incompatible with true rejoicing.

Religion turned sour can be far more crippling than no religion at all. A pagan can at least enjoy the good things of this life, whereas a puritan cannot. If the world tends to think of religion as drudgery, this may be because it sees too many dutiful 'older brothers'. The philosopher, Nietzsche, concluded that God was dead. His main evidence was the expression on the faces of so many believers: if their God were alive, surely they would look a little happier! How we deal with resentment is not a purely personal matter. Our credibility as believers is at stake.

A final line of reflection which the parable of the prodigal son might suggest for us touches on our experience of Church. How do we experience our membership of the Church? As we have seen, the elder brother was 'lost' at home, just like the lost coin. For some believers, the Church is like a safe vantage point from which they look out (and down!)

on a wicked world and its pleasures. For others, it is the home which they claim only reluctantly, and look at with a disapproval which closely mirrors that of the elder brother coming home from the field. Both righteousness and resentment can sour our sense of being at home in the Church. Either one can leave us 'lost at home', like the coin (Lk 15: 8-10) and the elder brother.

Revelation 13

This most dramatic of biblical texts can remind us that the decision to be a faithful disciple is one that will inevitably involve us in some drama. The majority of Christians today do not run any risk of literal, physical martyrdom, and we may never find ourselves in the situation of those for whom Revelation was written. However, Christian discipleship is no less radical an option today than it was for the earliest Christians. It is said that to be a Christian is to be recruited as well as redeemed. To choose Christ and his values is to reject much of what the world values. The effort to remain faithful to that choice involves an ongoing struggle with all that runs counter to it.

In our day-to-day living, we may not generally be aware of any great tension between our faith and the society in which we live. Yet there is an underlying, ongoing tension, and a very radical one at that. The believers in Nero's time could not but be aware of this tension. They were being forced into compliance with the values of the pagan world, under pain of economic exclusion and even death. The choice for them was utterly stark: apostasy or martyrdom.

For us, things are more subtle. The very absence of a radical choice may prevent us ever from choosing radically. Our discipleship can remain a comfortably complacent affair. Revelation 13 reminds us that Christian faith is a serious matter, calling at times for serious choices. Resistance is a part of our job-description as Christians. As the Second Letter to Timothy (3:12) puts it, 'all who want to live a godly life in Christ Jesus will be persecuted.' The 'persecution' may be no more dramatic than the on-going struggle to be honest, generous, chaste or forgiving, but this struggle can wear us down just as effectively as any physical threat. The rewards which the easier options hold out may not be as over-whelmingly enticing as the ones which compromise with Nero's regime promised, but in the long term, they may be just as tempting. What a tidal wave does not wash away, a steady trickle may wear away. As believers, we need to guard against the gradual attrition of our faith by secular values and attitudes.

Revelation 13 does not divide humanity into believers and unbelievers, or into religious and irreligious. The division which it makes is between true and false religion. Every human being will bow before something; it is impossible not to give our allegiance to some god or gods. Even when we are committed to God the Father, there may still be a certain polytheism operating in our hearts. Our reflection on Revelation 13 may invite us to examine our hearts and see where our deepest attachments lie.

During our *lectio* on this chapter, we saw that it is a very hopeful text. On the one hand, it acknow-ledges that believers will suffer, many of them unto death. On the other hand, it insists that such suffering is allowed by God as part of his design for salvation. The writer was concerned not to take the pain out of suffering, but to take the anxiety out of it. In his view, the one thing which faithful Christians need not suffer is anxiety. There is no room for doubt about the final outcome of the present struggle, since God, in Christ, has already defeated all the powers of evil.

In principle, all Christians share this outlook, but in practice, we often remain prone to anxiety, doubt and apprehension. It is very hard for us to leave things in the hands of God, even if we truly believe that he has created heaven and earth and everything in them (Gen 1:1ff.). Certainly, we are not asked to be fatalistic, or accepting of everything that comes our way. But the Lord who tells us to pray for our needs with perseverance tells us at the same time 'not to lose heart' (Lk 18:1).

St Paul was one believer who had come to full confidence in the victory of God. He did not arrive at this confidence easily or lightly, but through his experience of God's presence in his own struggles. Paul had run the gamut of suffering and anxiety (read 2 Corinthians 11:23-29!), but by the time he came to write the Letter to the Romans (his last epistle, even though it is the first of his letters we meet in the New Testament), Paul could say, 'For I am convinced that neither death, nor life, nor angels, nor rulers, nor things present, nor things to come, nor powers, nor height, nor depth, nor anything else in all creation, will be able to separate us from the love of God in Christ Jesus our Lord' (Rom 8:38-39). In retrospect, Paul could see that all that the Lord permitted him to suffer was an apprenticeship in trust and hope.

What about ourselves – closer, perhaps, to the apostles in the storm? We can at least take comfort from the very human weakness of these novices, with their anxious question, 'Teacher, do you not care?' (Mk 4:38). We might also reflect that the kind of trust which allays fear is something which we can choose to grow in. There can be a certain element of self-discipline involved in letting go of anxiety and taking hold of trust. It is a habit which we can actively cultivate. Every temptation to anxiety can be seen as an invitation to renew our trust, and to repeat, with the psalmist, 'I have calmed and quieted my soul' (Ps 131:2). The real battle which the Christians of the Book of Revelation faced was the inner struggle between hope and despair. They remind us that the greatest struggles in our own discipleship are played out, not in the world around us, but in the inner attitudes which shape our response to that world.

Oratio

In the progression between the different stages of *lectio divina*, the transfer from *meditatio* to *oratio*, from reflection to prayer, is the most spontaneous. Having read and understood the word of God, having reflected on it and seen how it speaks to us, it is only natural that we should react to what we have seen. When the penny drops, when we gain insight into how the word applies to our lives, we cannot but exclaim *eureka*! *Oratio*, or prayer, is nothing other than our reaction to the word. Of course, a very intense burst of insight is not the norm. Most of our encounters with the Bible will be much gentler, and the truth of the word will more often than not dawn slowly. Whether or not we feel that we have gained new insight from a given time of prayer with the word, we are called to renew our response to the word. God has spoken to us – now it is our turn to speak to God.

Although *oratio* is prayer in the strictest sense, we need to be fully convinced that all of our dealings with Scripture, from study onwards, are prayer in the broad sense. At the beginning of the book, when we reflected on prayer, we defined it in the broadest possible sense as *a relationship with God*. We are now considering it more specifically as our way of addressing God; as the way in which we speak to him. As we do this, let us bear in mind that the whole process of *lectio divina*, from beginning to end, is prayer.

How we pray is as personal and as individual as how each of us expresses him- or herself in any conversation. It follows from this that our description of *oratio* will be more tentative than was the case with *lectio* and *meditatio*. Nevertheless, there are some things that are – or should be – common to prayer, irrespective of the temperament or personality of the one praying, and in what follows we will try to outline some of these basic elements.

To say that the entirety of our discipleship and relationship with God is prayer, is to assert that everything we do is *implicitly* prayer. But as we remarked earlier, in order for everything we do to be prayer, there must be times when we do nothing but pray. To the extent that we try to live our lives as a response to God's grace, to his *deeds*, we are praying implicitly. When, in *oratio*, we deliberately and consciously respond to God's *words*, we are praying explicitly. Our times of explicit prayer ('nothing but prayer') are essential for sustaining a life of implicit prayer ('everything is prayer').

Let us review briefly the building blocks of *lectio divina* which we have so far encountered. In *lectio*, we look at the text from the outside, trying to understand it in an objective way. In *meditatio*, we continue our engagement with the text, but from the inside, no longer as observers but as protagonists. Now, in *oratio*, we give expression to whatever follows from our reading and reflection on the text. What happens to us when we enter deeply into a Scripture passage? In fact, one or more of many things. We may be struck by how far our lives are from the values and attitudes proposed by the text. In this case, a natural reaction would be to repent, to seek forgiveness, to resolve to strengthen our commitment. We might also be struck by the sheer goodness of God: by his mercy, his love, his providence, his power. If this is uppermost in our hearts, then the most natural reaction will be to praise and thank God. We may wish, having been struck by the goodness of God, to lay our personal needs, or the needs of loved ones, or of the world, before him with great trust. Here, our reaction to God's word in Scripture will spontaneously take the form of petition or intercession.

These three themes of repentance/resolve, thanksgiving/praise and intercession/petition, while not exhausting the possibilities for prayer, might be seen as a broad umbrella, covering the content of *oratio* (as a reflection on them, you might read or recite the Lord's Prayer, noting how the different elements of this prayer fall into one or other of these three broad divisions).

Consider any conversation between friends. The 'raw material' of a conversation is the sharing of news, joys, anxieties, struggles and hopes. In many conversations, we will wish to thank and praise a loved one, or to say 'I'm sorry.' In *oratio*, we do the same with God, as a response to his word. Our prayer is therefore a very natural, human response to his word. We do not need special expressions and formulas, because the 'language' of prayer is human language.

When our prayer is rooted in Scripture, the words we use may closely reflect or echo the language of Scripture. The prayer of Mary, the *Magnificat* (Lk 1:46-55), contains quotations from and echoes of at least 29 different passages from the Old Testament, most often from the Psalms. The Church's liturgical tradition takes up Mary's lead in praying responsorial Psalms, where we praise and thank God by reflecting back to him his own words. In the same way, in *oratio*, we may find it helpful to take a short verse or phrase from Scripture and repeat it (even throughout the day, while we are engaged in other activities). Phrases such as 'When the cares of my heart are many, your consolations cheer my soul' (Ps 94:19), 'Hope in the Lord' (Ps 131:3), 'Teacher, let me see' (Mk 10:51), 'Blessed be the God and Father of our Lord Jesus Christ (2 Cor 1:3), and countless others throughout the Bible, might also be used in this way. Just as in *meditatio*, where repetition of a verse can allow it to speak more deeply to our lives, so in *oratio*, repetition can help to anchor a biblical prayer more deeply in our heart.

We now turn once again to the three biblical passages which we have been using to 'practise' the stages of *lectio divina*. Again, we recall that our prayer needs to be our own, and this should be borne in mind as we read the suggestions for prayer which follow. For the sake of clarity, we will group these 'suggestions' under the three headings of repentance/resolve, thanksgiving/praise and intercession/petition. Note that praise and thanksgiving, while very close, are not identical. When we thank God, we have in mind what he has *done*. When we give praise, our focus is on God in himself: his qualities such as goodness, power and mercy. A distinction is sometimes made also between intercession and petition: we make intercession on behalf of others, whereas in the prayer of petition, we ask for ourselves.

Genesis 12:1-4

Repentance/resolve. Lord, you call us, just as you called our forefather Abraham. Our response to you can make a difference – not just to us, but to our families, our friends, our community and beyond. So often, Lord, we choose not to respond, but to cling to independence and autonomy rather than trusting obedience. We say, even if not in so many words, 'The devil I know is better than the God I can't see.' We opt for the anxiety of self-reliance, rather than the security which comes from complete trust. We busy ourselves with plans to build towers of our own, not taking time to discover the plan which you would have us follow. At times, we allow ourselves to be swallowed up by the doubt which is part and parcel of our human condition, rather than seeing it as an invitation to renew our trust in you.

You appeal, Lord, to the freedom you have given us. But how jealously we guard our freedom, forgetting that the greatest exercise of human freedom is commitment to you! Help us, Lord. Lead us from the isolation of independence to the warmth and security of a lived fellowship with you. May we make our own the words of the psalmist, 'The Lord is my shepherd, I shall not want' (Ps 23:1).

Thanksgiving/praise. We thank and praise you Lord, for you, the creator of heaven and earth, take a deep, personal interest in each one of us. You never force or coerce us, but wisely and gently use events, people and circumstances to reveal yourself to us. Your providence embraces all of reality. Nothing lies beyond your wisdom and power. Even tragedy and sin do not frustrate your loving plans, but can plunge us into the very heart of your mercy.

We give you thanks for those whose lives witness to the blessings that flow from trust in you, and for the courage of those who respond to you at great cost. These are the people who have kept faith alive and who continue to inspire us. They are the people whose lives make a difference, and whose example invites us to renew our confidence that 'truly God is good to the upright' (Ps 73:1).

Intercession/petition. Father, many of your children do not know you, or know you as a vague idea rather than as a loving parent. Give your light to those who struggle to find direction and meaning in life.

May they have a sense of your loving concern for them. Let them know that you have a plan for each of your children, and give them the faith and courage to open their lives to you.

Others, Lord, have lost their way. They have started with great trust in you, but their lives have taken them far from your light. May your call overtake them yet again, so that they may know once more the peace which comes from trust in you.

Help each of us to respond to you with great generosity, Lord. For we know that to do this is merely to let ourselves be blessed by your own generosity. Bless us with peace and perseverance as we follow you, for we know and we trust that 'the Lord watches over the way of the righteous' (Ps 1:6).

Luke 15:11-32

Repentance/resolve. Father, you depend on us, your children, to reach out to the lost, to welcome our brothers and sisters who feel alienated or excluded, to show your smiling face to those who fear only retribution and revenge. We, the body of your Son, are the arms that are to embrace the returning prodigal, restoring dignity and bandaging wounds. Too often, Lord, we have hardened our face, letting it be known that we cannot sympathise with those whose wounds are self-inflicted.

We repent, Lord, of any notion that we are virtuous. We repent of excessive reliance on our own efforts, especially where this has been at the cost of knowing our utter dependence on your grace. We thought that we were serving you, but you were gently and unobtrusively serving us. We repent of our presumption and lack of gratitude, and resolve to serve you in the most broken and needy of your children. Deliver us, Lord, from resentment and pride, as we pray, 'Who can detect their errors? Clear me from hidden faults' (Ps 19:12).

Thanksgiving/praise. Almighty God, we praise you for the marvellous depths of your wisdom. The words of Jesus shine right through our lives, lighting up patches of darkness which we had not even begun to suspect! We bless and praise you Lord, for you do not depart from us, nor leave us alone in our sinfulness. You do not turn aside from our petulance and our resentment, but draw ever closer to us, planting within us your word, which is a torch that burns our sinfulness away, even as it lights it up.

We thank you for the gentleness of your mercy. You continue to 'come out to us,' to find us where we are, whether near or far off. We encounter you in so many ways: a book, a homily, a letter, a chance meeting. The details of our lives conspire to lead us into the celebration, if we only have eyes to see you at work in them. May we learn to sing with gratitude, 'I will bless the Lord at all times; his praise shall continually be in my mouth' (Ps 34:1).

Intercession/petition. Lord, heal us of all bitterness, that we may not be a burden to our sisters and brothers. So many people bear within them an anger, which, silently and unobserved, eats away at their happiness like a deadly cancer. Protect us, Lord, when we meet such anger in others. In our weakness, we all too readily reflect it back to them. Give us instead the strength and gentleness to meet it with loving patience.

We dare, Lord, with confidence in your great mercy, to name even the anger which at times we can feel with you. Remove this and all bitterness from our hearts, leaving space there for us to share, as you have shared, the pain and suffering of others. Teach us to pray, and to lead others to pray, 'Bless the Lord, O my soul, and do not forget all his benefits – who forgives all your iniquity, who heals all your diseases, who redeems your life…' (Ps 103:2-3).

Revelation 13

Repentance/resolve. God our Father, your love for us is total, and so you call us in a total way. Your invitation extends to every aspect of our lives, and invites us constantly to make choices that are in keeping with our discipleship. Your call is radical, inviting us to choose radically. But we so often fail to take you seriously, opting instead for the false comfort of a half-response to your invitation. We leave room for response to other invitations, issued by other gods.

We are your fair-weather friends, Lord, loving you by half. We need not fear persecution, but the fear of inconvenience and effort leaves us open to seduction by other gods. We choose novelty rather than fidelity. Numb to the reality of sin and to our call to resist it, we sleep through the battles being played out around us between good and evil. We forget that we have been recruited as well as redeemed.

We resolve to work against our sluggishness, Lord, and to place all our hope in your victory over evil. May we take to heart the words of the psalmist, 'You have given me the shield of your salvation, and your right hand has supported me; your help has made me great' (Ps 18:35).

Thanksgiving/praise. Your word, Lord, assures us that you are in control – you have the whole world in your hands! For this we thank and praise you. Where we see suffering, injustice and every manner of evil, when we are confronted by our own sinfulness and inadequacy, we can take heart. Nothing lies beyond your influence; there is nothing that you cannot turn to our good. We thank you for the marvellous hope our faith gives to us. Even evil itself is taken up into your mysterious and totally effective plan.

The great pain and suffering present in the world confront us with our smallness and powerlessness, but your word comforts us, challenging us not to be overcome, but to overcome. Inner demons, too, may threaten to overwhelm us, but we need not fear them, for we have faith in your power and mercy. We praise your mighty power and thank you for the assurance of your constant help, as we say, 'God is our refuge and strength, a very present help in trouble. Therefore we will not fear, though the earth should change, though the mountains shake in the heart of the sea' (Ps 46:1-2).

Intercession/petition. God our Father, help us to appreciate how radical is the invitation to newness of life which you extend to each of us. May we know that our choice for you will often be a choice against false gods. Be with us, as we reject the gods of this world. Strengthen us in our resolve not to bow to pride, fear, power, pleasure, greed, comfort and ambition.

We pray for all who find the struggle of fidelity difficult. Lift up those who have fallen. Lead back those who have turned away. Renew those who feel tempted. Help all your people to discern your mighty hand at work even in the saddest and most desperate events of life. Let us never be overcome, but help each of us to grow steadily in trust, so that in every event we might pray, 'The Lord is my rock, my fortress, and my deliverer. My God, my rock in whom I take refuge, my shield, and the horn of my salvation, my stronghold' (Ps 18:2).

Contemplatio

In looking at *lectio*, *meditatio* and *oratio*, we have examined the heart of *lectio divina*. When we read a biblical text with understanding, reflect on its significance for our own lives, and then pray that we might live the message of the text, we have already done our utmost to ensure that the text will not return empty, but accomplish what God sent it to do (cf. Is 55:11). Some presentations of *lectio divina* end when they have looked at these three stages, and there is certainly a logic to such an approach. Generally speaking, the purpose of a description of *lectio divina* is to lead people to *do* it, to pray the Scriptures in this way. The three stages, reading, reflection and prayer, are *our effort* to make the message of Scripture our own, to let it sink deep within us and touch our lives. When we have engaged with a passage from the Bible through these three stages, there is – in a sense – not much more that we can do. The rest is God's work.

However, for just this reason, there is also a sense in which the work is only beginning when we have done our *lectio*, *meditatio* and *oratio*. The work of transformation is ultimately God's work. It is his grace which changes us, and the diligence with which we approach the Bible is simply our way of being open to the grace of God at work in us. For this reason, we can speak of a fourth stage in the process of *lectio divina*: the stage of *contemplatio*.

The English word 'contemplation' carries quite a lot of baggage with it, and is often misunderstood. We tend to think of contemplation as something done by contemplatives, which would be good reasoning, but for the fact that we generally restrict the term 'contemplative' to men and women living a monastic life. Furthermore, there is a common impression that contemplation is something extremely rare, and involves all sorts of strange 'mystical' experiences such as visions and ecstasies. It would be better to avoid thinking of contemplation in this way. It is not the exclusive preserve of monks and mystics, but rather, in the context of *lectio divina*, the logical next step after we have done our part to understand and pray the word of God.

Our intellect will take us only so far. When we are praying, our imagination and feelings may take us a little further. But after a certain point, we can do nothing other than let go and let God. When the well of reflection runs dry and we have said all that we can say, it is time to wait on the Lord! This is the beginning of contemplation. Our natural reaction, once we appear to have exhausted the possibilities for prayer with a passage or idea from the Bible, is to call it a day. It is not easy to sit in silence when there is nothing going on – or at least nothing that we can sense. But we need to give God a chance to work within us.

The paradox of contemplation is that while it is God's work, and as such calls for us to remain passive and receptive, there is perhaps nothing that calls for greater commitment and effort on our part than simply remaining still in God's presence. If contemplation is relatively rare, that is not because it is terribly high-flown, but because it is terribly ordinary. Some people who remain faithful to prayer over a long period of time may have remarkable experiences in contemplation, but for the most part, contemplation is nothing more – and nothing less – than remaining quietly and humbly in God's presence, allowing him to touch us.

Every time we do *lectio divina*, we should allow a period of time to put our Bible to one side and simply remain in silence. As often as not, this will be a time during which we struggle to achieve some inner stillness. It will not usually be a time of sweetness and light (if it were, presumably everyone would be doing it!), but a time during which we commit ourselves to being open, in faith, to what the Lord now wishes to say to us, and work within us. For this reason, we do not 'do' *contemplatio* on a given passage of Scripture: it is our effort to let God communicate with us directly.

How, given that it is God's work, do we 'do' *contemplatio*? It follows from what we have seen that our part is to let God do the work. In practice, this involves whatever we can do to be still in his presence. In practice also, *contemplatio* is more difficult than the other stages of *lectio divina*. As we noted while looking at prayer, it is often not easy to remain still. Our senses long for stimulation and our minds are full of noise. Many of the so-called 'meditation techniques' used in prayer (and in a purely secular context, for their health benefits and as a way of reducing stress) might more properly be called 'contemplation techniques,' since they are designed to help calm the mind. But whereas in secular meditation, the calming of the mind can be an end in itself, in the context of Christian prayer, we calm our mind in order to be receptive to God.

In Revelation 3:20, we read: 'Listen! I am standing at the door, knocking; if you hear my voice and open the door, I will come in to you and eat with you, and you with me.' In *lectio*, *meditatio* and *oratio*, the Lord knocks on the door of our hearts and minds. We might think of the famous painting by Holman Hunt, in which he depicts Christ, holding a lantern, knocking on a door which has no door handle. The artist explained that this was a deliberate omission, as the handle which would open the door to Christ was located on the inside of the door. The effort made to give our attention to the Lord in *contemplatio* is equivalent to turning the handle, located on our side of the door, in order to welcome him into our hearts and minds. All of our engagement with the word of the Lord has as its aim our transformation by the Lord of the word. *Contemplatio*, to the extent that it involves effort on our part, is our consent to this transformation.

Lectio divina and life

The word of God is for transformation rather than information. It is for life and for living. Likewise, *lectio divina* teaches us not just how to pray, but how to live. While we will need to devote specific times to it, *lectio divina* is not an activity which stands alone. The word of God cannot be a hobby or a special interest, but must touch our lives in a concrete and tangible way. Far from setting up a closed circuit, a cosy *tête-à-tête* between ourselves and God, praying the Scriptures opens us out, in a new and demanding way, to the world.

We could say that the word of God exercises two 'forces' on us. First, a centripetal force, which draws us in, fascinates us, involves us. But this is followed by a centrifugal force, which sends us back out, demanding that our lives proclaim the word we have encountered. The First Letter of St John expresses this clearly: 'What we have heard, what we have seen with our eyes, what we have looked at and touched with our hands, concerning the word of life… we have seen it and testify to it, and declare to you' (1:1-2). The test of authenticity in all our dealings with Scripture is the extent to which the word becomes flesh in the concrete circumstances of our lives.

Commitment to living the words of Scripture could be considered a fifth element in the process of *lectio divina*, because without it, the whole process would be radically incomplete. All those who take the Scriptures seriously are like the apostles, whom the Lord called 'to be with him,' and then 'to be sent out to proclaim the message' (Mk 3:14). Not all will be preachers, catechists or evangelists, but every believer is asked to carry the word to others, to be a missionary in his or her way of living. In the monastic tradition, two terms were used in reference to this 'outward' movement of the word. The word *communicatio* referred to an explicit sharing of the word with others (often in group sharing); the word *operatio* referred to the very concrete ways in which the word was put into practice. Our encounter with the word sends us out as communicators and operators, as proclaimers and doers of the word.

This dynamic of sharing the word is what motivates Mary to visit her cousin Elizabeth, immediately after the annunciation (Lk 1:26-40). Mary receives God's word from the angel, seeks to understand its meaning and its significance for her own life, and then consents to it: 'Let it be with me according to your word.' But the good news cannot be contained, and so the visitation follows the annunciation as night follows day. Traditional piety tends to focus on the kindness of Mary in going to the help of her cousin Elizabeth, who was six months pregnant; but the primary energy underlying Mary's visit is her wish – we might even say her need – to share the word and relate what God is doing in her life (Lk 1:46-55). If it were necessary to choose a single word to sum up the lived expression of *lectio divina*, it might well be *visitatio*,[2] or visitation. The 'annunciation' which is *lectio divina* demands that the lives of those who have received the word be a visitation to their brothers and sisters.

In conclusion, note that *lectio divina* is rather like a wheel turning full circle. Life and discipleship inevitably send us back to the word, for nourishment, consolation and wisdom. Our re-reading of the Scriptures in the light of experience can open ever-deeper levels of meaning in them.

Lectio divina and liturgy

Given our reflections on *lectio divina* up to this point, it might seem surprising to insist that the primary place where the Bible is read, reflected upon and prayed is not with the individual believer, but in the Church's liturgy. In practice, most praying with the Bible is done in private or in small groups, but the liturgy remains the place *par excellence* for breaking open the Scriptures. Although many liturgies can appear to be rather wordy affairs, with prayers, readings and reflections following each other in rapid succession, the fundamental 'business' of liturgical celebration (and in the Catholic tradition this applies above all to the Mass) is not word and speech, but *actualisation*, making the history of salvation, God's deeds on behalf of his people, *actually* present.

When Jesus led the liturgy of the word in the synagogue of his home town (Lk 4:16-21), he read from the prophet Isaiah, and then said: 'Today this scripture has been fulfilled in your hearing.' It is above all in the liturgy that the word of God becomes a *present* word, carrying out its purpose in our day. The word 'today' is a key word in the Bible, and it is the basis of all liturgical celebration. In the liturgy, we do not simply hear the word of God proclaimed, but are actually renewed as God's people, those who live by his word: 'You stand assembled today, all of you, before the Lord your God… to enter into the covenant of the Lord your God, sworn by an oath, which the Lord your God is making with you today; in order that he may establish you today as his people, and that he may be your God' (Deut 29:10, 12-13). In the liturgy, the demands of our covenant relationship with God are presented to us anew, not as a repetition of some ancient commandment, but as God's word to us *today*: 'O that today you would listen to his voice! Do not harden your hearts' (Ps 95:7). Again, in the liturgy, we are assured that the God who has worked wonders for his people in the past continues to show his love for his people in the present: the God 'who divided the Red Sea in two,' is the one whose 'steadfast love endures forever' (Ps 136:13).

The Bible is itself very much a liturgical book. From the beginning, the canon of Scripture was determined largely by the liturgy: only books which had been used regularly in the liturgy were finally accepted as canonical, that is, as part of sacred Scripture. Many of the biblical texts themselves originated in a liturgical setting (for example, Psalms, various hymns and canticles). Other biblical texts which did not actually originate in a liturgical setting were heavily influenced by liturgical concerns. An example of this is the Book of Revelation, which opens with the instruction that it be read in the assembly (1:3), and is full of references to the heavenly liturgy, which was reflected in the Church's liturgy. The letters of St Paul were intended to be read not individually, but in a communal setting. Often, this is clear from the opening verses of a letter, and it is made explicit in Colossians 4:16: 'When this letter has been read among you, have it read also in the church of the Laodiceans.'

Given that God speaks to his people *as a people*, and not primarily as isolated individuals, what is the relationship between *lectio divina* and the liturgy? It is an extremely close one – so much so that every celebration of the Mass is like a concentrated *lectio divina*, with the stages of *lectio divina* reflected clearly in the very structure of the Mass:

proclamation of the readings	*lectio*
homily	*meditatio*
prayer of the faithful	*oratio*
Holy Communion	*contemplatio*
dismissal	*'visitatio'*

The correspondence between Holy Communion and *contemplatio* becomes obvious as soon as we recall that both are times of transformation, in which Christ gives himself to us in order that we might become more like him. The Mass ends with a dismissal which is nothing other than a joyful command to go and visit our sisters and brothers with the Good News which we have heard and experienced in the liturgy. All that makes up our discipleship will then enrich, and be further enriched by, our next participation in the Mass. In the liturgy, as in personal prayer, *lectio divina* is like a wheel that turns full circle.

Despite the clear parallels, the fact remains that the Mass, as an exercise in *lectio divina*, is extremely concentrated – simply too concentrated to be intern-alised all at once. Therefore we need to dedicate time specifically to *lectio divina*, in order that we might appreciate and appropriate the full richness of the liturgy. Time spent in prayer before the Blessed Sacrament helps us to grow in appreciation of the Eucharist, and in a similar way, time spent in *lectio divina*, either individually or in small groups, helps us to appreciate, and enter into, the workings of God which we have celebrated in the liturgy.

A further, and very obvious, benefit of *lectio divina* is that it increases our familiarity with the Bible. The liturgy is not a Bible class, and it quite often presupposes a reasonable knowledge of Scripture. The quality of our participation in the liturgy can greatly increase as our knowledge of Scripture grows.

Sharing lectio divina

While *lectio divina* can give us a sound approach to personal prayer, it is also ideal for shared or group prayer. Even having a text read aloud by another person in a group can help us to hear it in a new way. A shared commitment to studying a text and understanding its background and meaning can make the effort involved more enjoyable. Alternatively, one individual in a group might undertake to study a particular passage or book, and share their findings with the group.

When it comes to *meditatio*, the benefits of sharing are very obvious, and at times it is quite amazing to hear how the word speaks so differently to different people. A period of common prayer or *oratio* can build up all who take part, and time allowed for silent *contemplatio* can keep everyone alert to the presence of the Lord, who assures us of his special action among people who come together to pray: 'Where two or three are gathered in my name, I am there among them' (Mt 18:20).

In practice, a group session of *lectio divina* could unfold as follows:

– Begin with a prayer, invoking the Holy Spirit, who has inspired the Scriptures, and who continues to work through them. In subsequent sessions, once the group has found its feet, the opening prayer could be followed by a period of sharing on how people have tried to apply or live out in their daily lives the passage of Scripture which was the focus of the previous session (note that in a prayer group of any kind, while everyone should be encouraged to share, it may be desirable to make it clear that nobody need feel obliged to do so);

– Read the chosen passage aloud, two or three times if it is not long (different readers!). Ideally, the members of the group will have known in advance what passage is being taken;

– Share any findings or insights that have been gained from study and reflection on the context of the reading;

– Share *meditatio*: what the text says to each member of the group in his or her life at present;

– Share a time of *oratio*: intercession, petition and praise (specific prayers of repentance may not always be appropriate in a group setting);

– Have a period of silence, for *contemplatio*.

– End the session with a set prayer, such as the Lord's Prayer, or the *shema*, Deut 6:4-7.

The total length of time may vary according to the

needs and circumstances of the group, but in general an hour will be the minimum length of time necessary, and it is probably best not to exceed this by much. From a practical point of view, it is best not to leave sessions open-ended, but to have a fixed finishing time.

We have now reached the end of our presentation of *lectio divina*, and the remainder of the book will be an application of what we have seen to the Gospel of Mark. Let us make the transition with a short biblical reflection on *lectio divina*.

Read Nehemiah 8:1-12. In this passage, Ezra the priest reads the Scriptures aloud in the assembly of the people. Ezra is charged with the task of leading a renewal of God's people, recently returned from exile. The exile was a tragic turn of events in their history, which the prophets insisted had resulted from the people's infidelity to their covenant relationship with God. Renewal and reconstitution as God's chosen people were to be based strictly on the word of God.

As you read through this passage, notice how the elements of *lectio divina* are contained in it. Pay attention also to the power of the solemn proclamation of the word of God, to the people's attentive listening, their understanding, their spoken response, their sorrow at the inconsistency between their lives and the word. Notice finally that the whole purpose of the proclamation is that they might experience the *joy* of living according to the word. Any sorrow that the word causes them is directed towards the joy of conversion and of renewed fellowship with God and with one another. Such transformation is the entire scope and purpose of *lectio divina*.

NOTES

1. I borrow this insight from Roland Meynet S.J., who presents it in his 1988 commentary on Luke's Gospel.
2. The Latin word *visitatio* fits in nicely with the other terms used in *lectio divina*, but note that in the Old Testament it can also have a negative connotation, such as in the Latin version of Hos 12:2, where it refers to God's intention to visit his anger on his people.

Part Three

Lectio divina with the Gospel of Mark

What is a Gospel?

While reflecting on Scripture, we took some time to clarify both what the Bible *is*, and what it is *not*. Let us now, more briefly, do the same for the Gospels. Instinctively, believers tend to think of the Gospels as mini-biographies, or lives of Christ. This is correct up to a point, but only up to a point. On the one hand, it is the Gospels that give us the information we have about the life of Jesus. Any further 'information' is a matter of speculation or pious imagination. On the other hand, however, the Gospels give us only limited information about the life of Jesus. They tell us nothing about his appearance; they give us no precise information regarding his date of birth; apart from a single episode (Lk 2:41-52), they pass over his childhood with a deafening silence. Where and by whom was he educated? Did he work with his father? Did he travel before beginning his public ministry?

If we are curious about the life of any famous person, we can read a biography. But the Gospels do not satisfy the curiosity which so many followers of

Jesus down through the ages have felt regarding his life. If they are biographies at all, they are so in a very limited and partial sense – so much so, in fact, that it may be better to avoid thinking of them as biographies in the usual sense of the word. Does this mean that they are not 'accurate' or 'true'? Not at all. But it does mean that we have to approach them with a different sensitivity and expectation than we would bring to a 'regular' biography.

The New Testament contains four Gospels.[1] All four recount the same overall story of Jesus of Nazareth, of his ministry and – especially – of his passion, death and resurrection. However, they each have their own specific concerns and emphases. Their details differ and – in a few places – even contradict each other. If we were to approach them as biographies, we would be forced to conclude that they can't all be right in every instance! Quite simply, then, the Gospels are a different type of literature to biography pure and simple. What, then, are they?

The Gospels have been described as *four portraits of Jesus*, and this is an excellent way of looking at them. If four talented artists were commissioned to paint portraits of the same individual, they would produce four different pictures. The subject would be recognisable from each one, and it would be largely pointless to ask which was the most accurate portrait. In each case, the artist's flair and style, along with his or her 'feel' for the person, would influence the work. In the case of the Gospels, the 'artists' have particular concerns in putting across their message. They are writing for specific communities, which need to hear different aspects of the life and message of Jesus emphasised, in keeping with their circumstances.

Concern to emphasise a particular aspect of Jesus' life or teaching does not lead to inaccuracy. To take a concrete example, someone sharing their faith in Jesus with a timid, scrupulous person will probably want to lay great stress on Jesus' tenderness and mercy. But another person, sharing their faith with someone who seems to be complacent or over-confident, may focus on the more challenging and demanding aspects of Jesus' teaching. This does not mean that there is an inconsistency between the two. They will simply be tailoring their words to the situations of their hearers. Far from falsifying Jesus or his message, they will be taking full advantage of the richness of the Christian faith. The four Gospels, with their different emphases, do not compete with each other for the most accurate picture of Jesus. Together, they enrich our understanding of him.

The Gospels have also been described as *sermons in story form*. They were originally composed from the very earliest sermons or homilies on Jesus and on the meaning of his life. A homily does not set out to deliver a blow-by-blow series of facts. It sets out not so much to *inform* as to *convince*. Certainly a good homily will be completely rooted in the facts about Jesus, but its whole purpose will be to nurture faith (rather than appeal to curiosity) in those to whom it is preached. As the Gospel of John puts it: 'these (things) are written so that you may come to believe' (20:31). The overriding concern which motivated the writers of the Gospels was to build up the faith of the Christian communities for which they were writing. This concern is built into the very fabric of the Gospels, and so these writings invite us to approach them with the overriding expectation that they will speak to our faith.

At this point, we might also ask why we should take a Gospel as our text for a longer exercise in *lectio divina*. The Gospels are the highpoint of the Bible. Since their subject matter is the life and teaching of Jesus, they have always been accorded special respect and reverence, even though Christians consider the entire Bible to be the word of God. The relationship between the Old and New Testaments has been described as one of *promise* to *fulfilment*. The very first Christians were Jews, familiar with the Old Testament and expecting that God would fulfil his promises to Israel. It was in the person of Jesus that they saw the definitive fulfilment of God's promises to Abraham (Gen 12:1-4), and of all the prophecies of the Old Testament. The Gospels are filled with quotations from and allusions to the Old Testament. From the very beginning, in fact, the disciples of Jesus were convinced that it was only in the light of their faith in Christ that they could fully understand the Old Testament (cf. Lk 24:13-35, where Jesus opens the meaning of the Scriptures to the two disciples on the road to Emmaus). Beginning *lectio divina* with a Gospel might also help to convince us of the value – indeed the necessity – of some familiarity with the Old Testament, for our understanding of the New.

A further reason for taking a Gospel as our text is that we will be on familiar ground. Hopefully, this will have the double advantage of alerting us to the risks which can be associated with excessive familiarity, while also ensuring that we feel somewhat 'at home' with the material we are reading and praying. We all have plenty of Gospel stories and teachings in our memories, and it will – again hopefully – be a useful exercise to approach old, familiar material in a fresh way.

Approaching the Gospel of Mark

Why the Gospel of Mark? We could, of course, have chosen any of the four Gospels, but there are several good reasons for choosing Mark at this point. Mark, to begin with, is the shortest of the four Gospels. To put the question of free time for Bible reading into perspective, it can be read through in the time it takes to watch a short television programme, or it can be read slowly and reflectively in the time it takes to watch a film! Mark also has a particular immediacy and urgency. The writer wastes no time in getting down to the details of Jesus' ministry and message. By the end of the first chapter, the reader has already seen Jesus preach, call disciples, cast out demons, cure all kinds of illness, and pray to his Father.

Mark's particular emphases drive home very effectively the nature of Christian faith and discipleship. As we shall see, he portrays the disciples as weak, unsteady individuals, slow to grasp the implications of following Jesus, and concerned to avoid sacrifice and suffering. He also portrays the humanity of Jesus in a most vivid way. Overall, Mark is at pains to make a point which we tried to stress earlier: that discipleship is not about doing wonderful things for God, but allowing God, who has, in his Son Jesus, embraced our humanity, to do wonderful things for us. Faith, prayer and discipleship are not for the competent and the strong: they are for those who share the ineptitude of the very first disciples, an ineptitude which Mark makes no attempt whatever to hide.

The purpose of Mark's Gospel

The four Gospels offer four distinct perspectives on the life and teaching of Jesus. Most believers do not distinguish between one Gospel perspective and another, having instead a general picture, drawn from all four Gospels. While it is good to have a 'whole' picture, there is a tremendous richness to be gained by examining each of the four Gospel perspectives in its own right. Naturally, a detailed examination would take a great deal of time and space, but we can illustrate the richness of the Gospels' diversity with a brief example.

Jesus is portrayed in very different ways in the Gospels of Mark and John. Mark stresses the humanity of Jesus, and his vulnerability to a whole range of sufferings. He experiences tiredness (4:38) and hunger (11:12). His ability to work miracles can be limited (6:5). There is something that he does not know (13:32). Perhaps most striking of all is that Mark shows us a Jesus who, in his time of greatest suffering, feels deserted by God, and cries out in despair: 'My God, my God, why have you forsaken me?' (15:34). In portraying Jesus in this way, Mark assures the readers and hearers of his Gospel that there is nothing they are suffering for their faith that Jesus himself has not endured before them.

The Gospel of John leaves us in no doubt about the humanity of Jesus, insisting on it from the opening verses: 'The word became flesh and lived among us' (1:14). But John's overall portrayal of

Jesus contrasts strongly with Mark's. Whereas Mark portrays Jesus as a servant, John portrays him as a king. In the fourth Gospel, Jesus is not the passive victim of his passion and death. He does not agonise in the garden of Gethsemane, but goes to his fate with complete serenity and in total control. He is killed not because he is weak, but because he has chosen to lay down his life (10:11). He is in complete control even at the moment of his death, not crying out in anguish, but bowing his head and giving up his spirit (19:30). The cry of abandonment from the cross which Mark includes in his Gospel would simply be out of place in the Gospel of John.

Why this difference between these two Gospels? It is because they are concerned with different situations in the lives of those for whom they are written. Like Mark's audience – indeed like all Christians – the believers for whom John writes need to have their faith strengthened, but John does this by underlining the fact that Jesus is indeed God's Son, and has been from the very beginning (1:1). Scholars offer many suggestions as to why John took this approach, but whatever about the details, the writer of this Gospel was convinced that the particular need of his audience was to hear the divinity of Jesus emphasised (while at the same time taking care to note that he was literally, and not just apparently, a flesh and blood human being, 19:34-35).

Which account is the most accurate, John's or Mark's? Hopefully, it will be clear by now that this question is redundant! The Jesus who was handed over to his enemies and experienced the full horror of suffering, fear and death is the same person who freely chose to give his life for our sakes. There is no contradiction between these two realities. As believers, there will be times when we take great comfort from the fact that Jesus has plumbed the depths of human experience. There will be other times when we will draw strength from the conviction that this same Jesus is truly the all-powerful Son of God. Looking further, there will be occasions when our deepest need is to ponder the gentle, merciful Jesus which Luke's Gospel so sensitively portrays, or the wise and authoritative teacher whom we meet in the Gospel of Matthew. The four Gospels provide us not so much with a single collage or pastiche, but with four complete pictures which complement each other in a way that hugely enriches the life of the Church and of the individual believer.

Returning to Mark, why did he write his Gospel? What is its principal purpose? Several concerns are reflected in the Gospel itself, but the one which predominates is the one which we have already noted: Mark's concern to encourage those who risk losing their faith because of difficult and painful circumstances. His portrayal of the weakness of the disciples in the face of suffering (for example, their flight at the arrest of Jesus, 14:50; Peter's fear which led him to deny knowing Jesus, 14:66-72) suggests that he was writing for a community which was undergoing or threatened by persecution. Some scholars suggest that he may have written his Gospel for Christians who had been or were being persecuted in Rome, under the mad emperor Nero. Whatever the exact historical circumstances, Mark spoke – and speaks – in a particular way to those whose faith is being put to the test by suffering.

Mark achieves his aim by showing that just as the sufferings of Jesus did not take from his identity as the Messiah, neither do the sufferings of his followers invalidate the faith which they have placed in Jesus. If the followers of Jesus are now being persecuted, or threatened with persecution, this does not mean that their faith has been an illusion. Faith in Christ does not shield one from suffering, because it is faith in a suffering Lord. This is why Mark gives so much attention to the sufferings of Jesus: if the Lord suffered greatly, his followers can hardly expect to escape suffering for their faith in him. In effect, Mark's Gospel is a comprehensive illustration of the words of Jesus in the Gospel of John: 'Servants are not greater than their master. If they persecuted me, they will persecute you' (15:20).

Almost from the beginning of Mark, Jesus is in conflict with the religious authorities of his time. In the space of a little over a chapter (2:1-3:6), there are no less than five episodes which mention the resentment and anger which was already building up against Jesus. The final episode ends with the ominous mention that the powers-that-be (both religious, represented by the Pharisees, and civil, represented by the Herodians) are planning to kill Jesus. The cross, which will completely dominate the end of Mark's Gospel, has been anticipated almost from the beginning. The life of Jesus, and of his followers, will be lived in its shadow.

The first disciples, as Mark portrays them, resist the cross. They fail to see how the Messiah could be destined to suffer, and they refuse to countenance the idea. Mark wants the readers of his Gospel to see themselves reflected in the fear and confusion of

Jesus' earliest followers. He also wants to draw a parallel between the experience of Jesus and that of his followers. Jesus, God's beloved Son (1:11), experienced every kind of opposition and suffering. But his sufferings were not the end, and he was vindicated in the resurrection. When the followers of Jesus experience great suffering, this does not mean that they have been deceived or forsaken by God – even if that is just how things appear. For Jesus' disciples, suffering is not the end, but the path marked out by Jesus himself, which he himself trod on his way to glory. Having said this, we should also note that the sufferings of disciples are not equivalent to those of Jesus. Only the sufferings of the Messiah, God's Son, could win salvation. Those who follow the pattern of his life will participate in the salvation which could have been won by no-one but Jesus.

Why should Mark have felt the need to stress all of this? He was writing for people who were already Christians. Surely they knew the story of Jesus, and could hardly have expected to swan through life without some share in his sufferings? We need to remember that the story of Jesus was still very new. The early Christians will have been convinced that their faith in Jesus was the way to salvation, but their understanding of their faith may not have been very mature. Some of them, having been baptised with great fervour and enthusiasm, may well have entertained rather glorious notions of what discipleship entailed in the present (again, rather like the earliest disciples, cf. Mk 10:37). If the disciples for whom Mark wrote his Gospel had any sort of honeymoon period at the beginning of their walk with Jesus, they are now being faced with some of the harsher aspects of fidelity to him. Mark leaves them with little doubt that the glory of discipleship lies in the future, and that the path to it passes over Calvary.

What scholars sometimes refer to as a 'theology of glory' may actually have been a common mistake in the earliest days of Christianity – and an understandable one at that. It is to be expected that the earliest Christian converts would have more enthusiasm than insight. Filled with the joy and zeal of any new convert, their first experience of real suffering for the Gospel will have come as a tremendous shock. Therefore, part of Mark's task will have been to educate and temper their expectations. Nobody, the first disciples included, could fully understand Jesus before, or aside from, his passion and death (cf. Mk 9:9). Mark drives home this point by highlighting the apostles' persistent inability to understand Jesus during the course of his ministry. Only after the experience of the cross are they enlightened regarding Jesus' identity as the suffering Messiah. *Per crucem ad lucem*!

Beginning to read Mark

At this point, and before proceeding any further, it would be well to take the time to read the Gospel of Mark, bearing in mind what we have seen about Mark's purpose in writing his Gospel. If possible, it is best to read the entire Gospel through at a single sitting. This helps to give an overall feel for the Gospel.

Having read through Mark, it is time to begin our exercise in *lectio divina*. As with the three 'sample' texts we looked at earlier, we will do exercises in *lectio*, *meditatio* and *oratio*. The concern of each of these three stages can be recapped and summed up by a question:

– In *lectio* we ask, '*What does the text say in itself?*'
– In *meditatio* we ask, '*What does the text say to me?*'
– In *oratio* we ask, '*What does the text lead me to say?*'[2]

Commentaries on the Gospel of Mark are generally far longer than this book, and in what follows we are necessarily limited in the amount of attention we can give to explaining the text. We cannot work our way systematically through the Gospel, offering an explanation or *lectio* of each passage. Instead, we will look at ten aspects of Mark, in an order which, while not keeping strictly to the order of Mark, will have a certain logic. A library could be filled with writings on this Gospel alone, and we will have achieved a great deal if we can draw out – and respond to – just some of what Mark has to say to our experience of discipleship.

1. Good news!

Lectio. 'The beginning of the good news[3] of Jesus Christ, the Son of God.' These are the words with which Mark opens his portrait of Jesus. We have already begun our *lectio* on Mark's Good News, and it may be helpful to refer back, from time to time, to what we have said about Mark's audience and his overall purpose in writing. We might notice straight away that there is an element of tension between Mark's unrelenting portrayal of suffering on the one hand, and the very idea of Good News on the other. How can a story of opposition, misunderstanding, betrayal, agony and death be considered good news?

The answer lies in the identity of Jesus: he is the Son of God, come among us, walking with men and women. In him, God reaches out to humanity as never before. This is clear from the short episode of Jesus' baptism, in 1:9-11. Jesus approaches John, asking for the 'baptism of repentance for the forgiveness of sins' (1:4). The sinless Son of God begins his ministry by placing himself firmly on the side of sinners. When Jesus does this, something wonderful happens: the heavens open, and the voice of the Father exclaims, 'You are my Son, the Beloved; with you I am well pleased' (1:11).

In fact, there are two places in the Gospel where we find Jesus totally identified with sinners. Here, and at the time of his crucifixion (15:22ff.). According to the Bible, crucifixion, being 'hung on a tree', was a sign that a person was 'under God's curse' (Deut 21:23). Crucifixion was *the* death for the sinner. Near the beginning of the Gospel, Jesus undergoes the baptism of sinners. Near its end, he dies the death of sinners. On each occasion, the distance between God and humanity is bridged: the first time, in anticipation; the second time, in fact. Mark tells us that as soon as Jesus was baptised, he saw the heavens '*torn* apart', and that as soon as Jesus died, 'the curtain of the temple was '*torn* in two, from top to bottom' (15:38). At the time of Jesus, it was believed that God lived above the heavens, which was a way of affirming that he was totally 'other', at an infinite distance from his creation. In order for him to visit humanity, the heavens would need to be torn. This is what lies behind the cry in Isaiah 64:1, 'O that you would tear open the heavens and come down.' At the baptism of Jesus, God begins his answer to this ancient prayer.

At the moment of Jesus' death – a death for sinful humanity – the temple curtain was torn. This was the barrier separating the holiest part of the temple in Jerusalem (for the Jews, the holiest place on earth, the place of God's very presence) from the rest of the temple complex. Nobody, under pain of death, was permitted to pass behind this curtain, the sole exception being the high priest, and he could do so on just one day in the year. Jesus' death on the cross, his final and complete identification of himself with sinful humanity, tore apart the barrier separating people from God. What was signalled at the time of his baptism in the river Jordan was accomplished at the time of his second 'baptism' (in 10:38, Jesus had referred to his death as a baptism. This important verse underlines the connection between his baptism by John and his death on the cross).

This is why Mark is Good News, even though so much of this Gospel is given over to suffering and death. The Good News is that through the sufferings of Jesus, the obedient one, the relationship between God and humanity, fractured by disobedience, is restored. In Jesus, there is a new beginning, the restoration of God's creation, the 'salvation' of all that had been captive to disobedience (note that the words 'the beginning' of Mark 1:1 echo the words 'in the beginning' of Genesis 1:1, as do the opening words of the Gospel of John).

This is the Good News which Jesus preaches

(1:14-15). It is the news for which people will leave everything – house, brothers, sisters, mother, father, children, fields (10:29); the news which is to be preached to the whole world (13:10; 16:15).

Meditatio. What is good news for us? What brings a smile to our face? What is the good that we would wish for our loved ones? Mark reminds us that our natural, instinctive outlook may not be the only or the best way of looking at reality. The very best things can come out of suffering, like the beautiful serenity we sometimes see in the expression of a person who has suffered greatly, or the depth of compassion we meet in someone who knows our pain because they have 'been there'. Mark's Good News challenges our superficiality, and invites us to see – with the eyes of faith – beneath the surface of things.

The love of God can transform even the most desperate tragedy into a blessing. Where has God 'broken into' our lives? What events has he used to tear through the barriers between ourselves and him? Of course, he uses all events, if we have faith to see him at work. But as we reflect on our lives, we will see, in all likelihood, that God has a special way of using the more difficult events of life to get through to us. In Jesus, God has redeemed suffering itself, giving it a new value and a new dignity.

The Father delights in seeing his Son take our side. We can be sure that he delights in seeing us taking his Son's side. There is a new beginning waiting for us, whenever we renew our commitment to Jesus, which is to do nothing other than open up to the one who has committed himself totally to us. We should not turn away from the Lord on account of weakness or sinfulness. Jesus does not shun us on this account. He is greater than the good man of Psalm 1, who does not 'take the path that sinners tread' (v. 1). Although sinless, he has identified himself completely with the sinner, and carried the burden of our sinfulness.

Oratio

Repentance/resolve. Father, we can never adequately thank you for your love – but we can try! Forgive our slowness to appreciate 'the breadth and length and height and depth' (Eph 3:18) of the love which you have shown us in your Son Jesus. Forgive our failure to place ourselves on the side of the weak and the suffering. Help us to trust more in your tremendous love, so that we do not shy away from beginning anew as often as we must.

Thanksgiving/praise. Long ago, Lord, you told your people: 'You are precious in my sight, and honoured, and I love you, I give people in return for you, nations in exchange for your life' (Is 43:4). Now, in Jesus, you have given your very self to all nations! May our lives and our lips thank you for the greatness of your love. We praise your great wisdom, which drew the blessing of salvation from the death of your Son. We thank you for the hope our faith in Christ holds out to us, that every human suffering, even death itself, finds meaning in his cross.

Intercession/petition. Give your light, Lord, to all those whom you have called to preach the Good News of Jesus. Be with missionaries, catechists and parents.

May their lives be good news to others. Console and strengthen those who struggle to discern good news in the events of their lives. Sustain them; give them eyes of faith to see the cross of Christ where eyes of flesh see only pain. May all your people learn to pray with confidence: 'Blessed be the God and Father of our Lord Jesus Christ, the Father of mercies and the God of all consolation' (2 Cor 1:3).

2. The unexpected Messiah – the unlikely King

Lectio. Take a moment to read the following verses in Mark: 1:25, 34, 44; 3:12; 5:43; 7:36; 8:26, 30; 9:9. Jesus' repeated reluctance to let his identity and power be seen by everyone does not seem to rest easily with the notion that he is bringing Good News for all to hear. Why is he so concerned to flee the limelight and conceal his power and identity? Up to a point, the answer is obvious: if word about Jesus' ability as a healer and exorcist 'gets out,' he will be mobbed. He will have no time and space to preach the Good News, which is the reason he came in the first place. We can see this beginning to happen already in chapter 1, where the disciples tell Jesus that everyone is looking for him, but he insists that he must go and preach elsewhere (vv. 37-38). Jesus has not come to bring people a 'quick fix,' to solve all their problems by a marvellous display of power. The healings and other miracles he works point ahead to what he wishes to do for all of humanity, but they are a signpost rather than a shortcut. There was a risk that people, on seeing Jesus' power, would get the wrong impression about him, and fix their hope on him in a superficial way.

There is another, more important, reason for Jesus' coyness about his identity. The reader of Mark is told from the beginning that Jesus is the Christ, the Messiah.[4] This information is intended to guide how we will read the Gospel: that is, with the expectation that it will tell us what kind of Messiah Jesus is. However, for the people whom Jesus met in the course of his ministry, the order was just the opposite. They needed to come to know what kind of person Jesus was *before* hearing that he was the Messiah. If Jesus had revealed his identity as Messiah from the beginning of his public life, he would have been completely misunderstood.

As Christians far removed in time from the actual events, we know that Jesus is the Messiah and Son of God, and that he died for us. But if the only thing we had ever heard about him was that he was the Son of God, we would most certainly not have expected him to die, less still to die the death of a criminal in order to save us from sin.

In Jesus' time, there was an expectation among the Jews that God would send a Messiah. This figure would deliver God's people from every form of oppression and slavery, just as had happened at the time of the exodus from Egypt. Overall, the expectation was that the Messiah, when he arrived, would exercise great political and even military clout. He would rout the hated Romans, whose presence made the Jews feel like exiles in their own land. In him, God would finally and definitively save his people.

Jesus, of course, had much in common with this expected figure. He was indeed God's anointed, the Messiah. He had been sent to free God's people from every form of slavery. In him, God's salvation of his people would be complete. But there was also much about Jesus that was entirely unexpected. The slavery which concerned him was not so much political oppression, as slavery to sin. He had come not only to save the Jewish people, but all of humanity. Most importantly, he would not exercise political and military power to bring about salvation. His weapon would be the instrument of his passion: not swords or knives, but the cross.

Jesus, then, is the *unexpected* Messiah. He cannot reveal his identity until it is fully clear to people that he will not be taking the road of power and resistance. We, the readers of the Gospel, are privileged to hear from the first verse that he is both Messiah (Christ) and Son of God. The next time these titles are used together is when the drama of the passion is well underway, and Jesus is being interrogated by the high priest: 'Again the high priest asked him, "Are you the Messiah, the Son of the Blessed One?" Jesus said, "I am"' (14:61-62). It is only when Jesus has fully shown his hand as the *suffering* Messiah that it is safe for his identity to be plainly revealed. Earlier in the Gospel, Peter had come to realise that Jesus was the Messiah (8:29), but Jesus had forbidden him to repeat this, since he knew that Peter's understanding was still incomplete.

Jesus, Messiah and Son of God, is also a *king*. Many of the Jews will have expected the Messiah to be a king, and so once again, Jesus might appear to fit the bill. Again, however, his kingship is hidden and unexpected – so much so, that like his Messiahship, it cannot be revealed until his passion. Then it is proclaimed repeatedly, even if unwittingly, by his enemies (Mk 15:2, 9, 12, 18, 26, 32). In Mark's

Gospel, Jesus, the hidden king, proclaims his hidden kingdom. The kingdom of God is actually a very important theme in this Gospel: the fact that this hidden kingdom has come near in the person of Jesus is the heart of the Good News (1:14-15).

Just what *is* the kingdom of God, as proclaimed by Jesus? From Jesus' own words, we know that it is something that calls people to repentance (1:15), and that it develops in a way that is hidden and unobtrusive (4:26), but powerful (4:30-32). Jesus tells us also that this kingdom needs to be accepted with the simplicity and vulnerability of a child (10:14-15), and that those who are wealthy and self-sufficient will have great difficulty entering into it (10:23-25). Yet nowhere does Jesus state simply and directly what the kingdom of God *is*. He is content to tell us what it is *like*, and then leave us to discover it for ourselves. The most important thing to note is that the kingdom of God does not have any geographical boundaries. It is not confined to a specific place or territory. The closest we come to a definition of it is actually in the Gospel of Matthew, where Jesus teaches his followers to pray, 'Your kingdom come, your will be done' (Mt 6:10). These two short phrases are in strict parallel with each other: wherever God's people are doing his will, there God reigns. And wherever God reigns, there is his kingdom.

As we shall see, even the apostles, Jesus' closest followers, were extremely slow to appreciate that Jesus was not proclaiming a kingdom of worldly power, prestige and glory. It dawned on them only gradually that those who follow this most unconventional of kings must expect to receive a cross before receiving a crown.

Meditatio

What are our expectations as followers of Christ? What effects, if any, do we expect our discipleship to have in our lives? It is good to have expectations, even if not all of them are fully correct. Many of Jesus' earliest disciples needed to have their expectations corrected, and even if this was a slow and painful process for them, it yielded great fruit in their lives. For many believers, faith becomes predictable and routine. They do not expect anything new under the sun; they become closed to the possibility that God might want to bring about something really new in them. Perhaps it is better to have hopes and expectations tempered by experience than not to have any at all. If we trust in the Lord, should we not also expect to receive good things from him? If we can be surprised at how the Lord permits suffering, might there not also be room for surprise at how he can bring joy? We might take encouragement in this from the words of the Psalmist: 'My soul longs, indeed it faints for the courts of the Lord; my heart and my flesh sing for joy to the living God' (Ps 84:2).

The hiddenness of Jesus' kingship and of his kingdom is both a challenge and a consolation to us. It challenges our thirst for novelty, reminding us that all that glitters is not gold. At the same time, it consoles us with the insistence that it is precisely in the ordinariness of life that the Lord is at work. Discipleship does not involve a fanfare: the seeds planted within us at our baptism and through our hearing of the word grow in a quiet way, but will produce a harvest if we try to remain faithful to the Lord in our daily lives.

Jesus did not want his earliest followers to latch onto his miracles and be filled by them with a superficial enthusiasm. Our rational culture does not encourage us to interpret any of the events of our lives as miracles, and this may not be such a bad thing. However, it is also no bad thing to cultivate an awareness of how the Lord has blessed and continues to bless us. The blessings which we enjoy do not *prove* our faith, by they can certainly *improve* it, if we try to see them through the perspective of what faith we have.

Oratio

Repentance/resolve. Lord, we believe in you. We believe that you have given yourself unreservedly out of love for us. And yet this conviction can so often remain ossified and stale, as though your wonders for us ceased on the cross. Help us to expect further wonders, to believe that your love is still active in our lives, in the most concrete, if unexpected, of ways. Give us eyes to see your hands at work around us. Give us a heart and a will to be those hands for others. May we make our own the wise conviction of the prophet: 'Even youths will faint and be weary, and the young will fall exhausted; but those who wait for the Lord shall renew their strength, they shall mount up with wings like eagles, they shall run and not be weary, they shall walk and not faint' (Is 40:30-31).

Thanksgiving/praise. We thank you, Lord, for your wonderful gentleness, which does not sweep us along, but leaves us free to discern your workings in our lives. Your love for us is, in the words of a hymn, 'as gentle as silence'. Your presence is as hidden as your kingdom, yet just as powerful. You walk with us, as you walked with the disciples on the road to Emmaus, with gentle respect for our limited understanding and partial grasp of things. With grateful hearts we affirm that you are the one who 'lifts up the soul and makes the eyes sparkle,' who 'gives health and life and blessing' (Sirach 34:20).

Intercession/petition. Gentle Lord, at times your silence becomes a burden to us, and we want to say with Moses: 'Show me your glory, I pray' (Ex 33:18). Be with all those who struggle to discern your presence in their lives; with those who have lost any sense of your presence; with those who cannot see the signs of your kingdom around them. Be the strength of all who pray: 'Hear, O Lord, when I cry aloud, be gracious to me and answer me! "Come," my heart says, "seek his face!" Your face, Lord, do I seek. Do not hide your face from me' (Ps 27:7-8).

3. Mark's very human portrait

Lectio. None of the four Gospels leaves us in any doubt that Jesus is fully human, flesh and blood. A concern behind some passages in the Gospels (especially in John) is to correct the false notion that Jesus was not actually a flesh and blood person, but that he merely *appeared* to be so. The Gospel of Mark portrays the humanity of Jesus in a clear and at times striking way – so much so that the Gospels of Matthew and Luke, both of which use a lot of the material found in Mark,[5] tend to tone down Mark's very human portrayal of Jesus. Even after two millennia of Christianity, many believers accept the humanity of Jesus only in theory. They remain uncomfortable with the idea that Jesus was fully human, like the rest of humanity in all things but sin (cf. Heb 4:15). For this reason, it may be worthwhile to linger for a moment on Mark's very human portrait of Jesus.

We have already noted some of the human limitations of Jesus: his susceptibility to fatigue and hunger, his capacity even to feel despair. A further emotion which Mark notes is Jesus' pity or compassion (1:41): Jesus is personally touched by the sufferings of others. Less positive, and therefore more surprising, emotions which Jesus shows in Mark's Gospel are anger, indignation, frustration – even a hint of irritation. Most famously, Jesus' anger is clear when he drives dealers and sellers from the Temple in Jerusalem (11:15-17). He is also angered by the legalistic stubbornness of the Pharisees, who considered that strict Sabbath observance should take priority over restoring someone to fullness of life (3:5).

In 8:12, it is again the Pharisees who provoke a reaction of weary frustration from Jesus, who sighs deeply as he criticises them for demanding signs. But it is his own disciples who provoke the most intense expression of Jesus' frustration (reminding us, perhaps, that like the rest of us, Jesus was freer in his criticism of those whom he loved most!). Shortly after the second miracle of the loaves in Mark's Gospel, the disciples are fretting about not having enough food with them. Jesus is dismayed that having witnessed his miracles, they can still be worried about food. He launches a tirade of questions at them (seven questions in quick succession), in an effort to shame them into greater trust in his providence (8:14-21). In this episode, we see in Jesus something of the frustration of a brilliant teacher who is stuck with the slowest of pupils.

Focussing on the humanity of Jesus does not take from his greatness in any way. On the contrary, it highlights the extraordinary love and mercy of the one who, 'though he was in the form of God, did not regard equality with God as something to be exploited, but emptied himself, taking the form of a slave, being found in human form' (Phil 2:6-7). The full humanity of Jesus is nowhere more clear than in the horror he felt at the prospect of suffering and death. Being the Son of God did not free him from the human reaction of pleading that he might be spared torment, and he was, by his own admission, 'scared to death' at the thought of what lay ahead of him (Mk 14:32-36). It was only his love – for his Father and for men and women – that gave him the strength to pass through this trial. And so St Paul continues his reflection: 'Being found in human form, he humbled himself and became obedient to the point of death – even death on a cross' (Phil 2:7-8).

Meditatio. The teaching of Jesus is a light for all people of good will. It is 'a lamp to our feet and a light to our path' (cf. Ps 119:105). Yet Jesus himself does not fit into neat categories. He is greater than any ideas we may have about him. It would be easy, and it can be tempting, to 'solve' the mystery of Jesus, by fixing on either his divinity or his humanity, instead of holding both together, as the great mystery that they are. In practice, it can be all too tempting to solve the mystery by glossing over the humanity of Jesus, but the Gospel of Mark certainly gives us no such freedom. Jesus, the unexpected Messiah and King, is unexpectedly human. He has come not to save us *from* but *through* our humanity. The human nature which God created is the raw material through which he has redeemed us in his Son.

In New Testament times, many pagan religions understood salvation as the act or process of being freed *from* our created human nature. In this outlook, creation was a mistake, and salvation meant the undoing of this error. This is not the biblical outlook, which insists (repeatedly!) that God created all things good, and the human person was the highpoint of his craft (Gen 1:26-31). What God affirmed at the creation of man and woman, that his creation was very good, he spoke with infinite care in the incarnation: human nature was not, of itself, an obstacle to his working. It was good enough for his Son, Jesus.

We tend, all too lightly, to drive a wedge between what is human and what is holy, between the human and the spiritual, the human and the saintly. This can have the unfortunate effect either of cheapening God's creation, or of making holiness appear irrelevant. Mark's portrayal of Jesus, with all his human feeling and vulnerability, invites us to value our human nature, and to see it as a gift from God. Of course, our humanity is weak and fallen. We need God's grace, the nourishment of his word and the support of the Christian community. But our human nature is not, in itself, the problem. It is our nature under the power of sin and selfishness that breaks our relationship with God. Christ, our human saviour, came not to cancel out, but to renew our humanity. All of our emotions, energies and gifts can be brought into his service. All of our failings can be brought to his mercy... 'For we do not have a high priest who is unable to sympathise with our weakness, but we have one who in every respect has been tested as we are, yet was without sin. Let us therefore approach the throne of grace with boldness, so that we may receive mercy and find grace to help in time of need' (Heb 4:15-16).

Oratio

Repentance/resolve. Pardon us, O Lord, for our impatience with ourselves, for the desire which we sometimes feel to stamp 'return to sender' on the human nature which you have given to us. You invite us to put all our energies into being good news for others, and to see our weakness as a highway to your mercy. Perhaps a little too often, we have invested much strength into fretting about our weakness. This nature of ours is the nature which you took to yourself. May we treasure it, and accept our creaturely limitations. May we love and serve you as you have asked us to: with all our heart, all our soul, all our mind and all our strength (Mk 12:30).

Thanksgiving/praise. We praise you Lord, for you have not disdained the weakness of human nature, but have embraced it fully. We thank you for giving us the hope that you can work not only through our strengths and abilities, but also through our limitations, if we will only entrust ourselves to you with confidence. How well the words of the prophet apply to you, Lord: 'A bruised reed he will not break, and a dimly burning wick he will not quench; he will faithfully bring forth justice' (Is 42:3).

Intercession/petition. Grant healing and renewal, Lord, to those who have lost confidence in themselves and in their ability to be a blessing to others. May they find their strength in you, and recover a sense of their worth in your eyes and of their value to others. May all your people put themselves fully in the service of their brothers and sisters, and so help to advance your kingdom. May we rejoice in each other's giftedness and support each other in our weakness. Grant us to live as you have shown us to: 'with all humility and gentleness, with patience, bearing with one another in love' (Eph 4:2).

4. Jesus, worker of miracles

Lectio. Of the four Gospels, Mark devotes the greatest proportion of his story to the miracles of Jesus. This might seem to be at odds with the idea that Jesus is a suffering Messiah, and not someone who will wield power in a very obvious way. In fact, Mark does not use the miracle stories to try to prove the identity of Jesus as the Son of God. They are not attention-getting devices, and they do not, of themselves, lead people to faith in Jesus. All in all, miracles are meant more to stimulate questions about Jesus, than to provide answers about him (Look, for example, at the reactions which miracles provoke in Mark 1:27; 6:52).

The miracle stories in the Gospels work at two levels. At a surface level, they show the power of God working for his people in various concrete ways, ranging from healing them to feeding them. At a deeper level, the miracles have a powerful symbolic meaning. The exorcisms (for example, Mk 1:23-26) are not just about the deliverance of individuals from captivity to evil spirits: they are an anticipation and a promise of the complete victory of God over all the powers of evil.

Likewise, the healings which Jesus works have a significance beyond the individuals who directly benefit from them. When Jesus cures a leper (1:40-45), he restores him not just to health, but to membership of the community. Lepers were outcasts, untouchables. The most painful part of their condition was the isolation which it imposed on them. In healing them, Jesus is making plain his concern that people be in community rather than in isolation. Similarly, in healing a paralytic (Mk 2:1-12), Jesus is not simply restoring a person's mobility. Beyond this obvious change was the symbolic restoration of someone's ability to follow Jesus himself. In the religious language of Jesus' time, the action of walking was taken as symbolic of how one lived as a moral or religious person. To be faithful to God was to 'walk blamelessly' (Ps 15:2), to 'walk in his ways' (Ps 81:13). The opposite was to refuse 'to walk according to his law' (Ps 78:10). Against this background, restoring someone's ability to walk had an obvious symbolic meaning.

Perhaps the most powerfully symbolic of the miracles in Mark's Gospel are Jesus' two healings of blind people. In the next section we will see that these are altogether more than just physical healings, but point to the opening of people's eyes to the nature of discipleship.

One episode in Mark clearly underlines the fact that the miracles are to be seen at a deeper level than their obvious physical character. This is the passage where Jesus is asked to come and cure a dying child, and the story is interrupted by the account of another healing (5:21-43). The healing of the woman with a haemorrhage is 'sandwiched' into the story of the raising of the dead child. This is not the only place in the Gospel where Mark has inserted one story into another one, and where Mark does this, he wants us to interpret the middle story in the light of the story into which he has squeezed it. In this case, the healing of the woman with a haemorrhage is to be seen as somehow equivalent to a raising from the dead. On account of her illness, the haemorrhaging woman would have been treated much like a leper – unclean and untouchable. This is why she is so furtive in approaching Jesus. In healing the woman's flow of blood, Jesus is also healing her alienation from society. For Jesus, to bring someone 'in from the cold' in this way, to restore them to communion with others, is equivalent to bringing them from death to life.

There is another type of miracle which has an almost totally symbolic meaning, and that is where Jesus exercises miraculous control over nature. The first such miracle we encounter in Mark is the calming of the storm on the lake (4:35-41). Jesus is sleeping peacefully in the boat, while the disciples are beginning to panic. In calming the waters, Jesus demonstrates the kind of power that God exercised over the waters of chaos at the moment of creation (Gen 1:2). Only God himself can exercise this sort of power, and so this miracle points to the hidden nature of Jesus.

Something similar is the case in 6:45-52, where Jesus walks on the water. He does this not in order to impress the apostles with his marvellous ability, but to show them that he is bringing about something radically new, just as God did in bringing his people out of slavery, through the waters of the Red Sea. Before long, the followers of Jesus would begin to understand that Jesus himself was 'the Lord, who makes a way in the sea, a path in the mighty waters,' and who says: 'I am about to do a new thing; now it springs forth, do you not perceive it' (Is 43:16, 19).

Closely tied up with Jesus' walking on the water is the miracle of the loaves (this comes just before the walking on the water, in Mk 6:30-44). These two miracles are not joined together by accident. They are joined in the same way as the crossing of the Red Sea is joined to the miracle of the manna in the desert (Ex 16:1-21). At the time of the exodus, God exercised power over the waters of the sea, and then fed his people with manna from heaven. In the same way, Jesus, who is leading people in a new exodus, feeds the people whom he has gathered together in a deserted place (Mk 6:35), and immediately afterwards reveals his power over the waters. Little wonder that the first Christians were quick to connect these two episodes to baptism and the Eucharist. In baptism, believers pass through water from captivity to sin to faith in Christ. In the Eucharist, they are nourished by Christ himself.

Meditatio

Having seen that there is more to Jesus' miracles than meets the eye, perhaps we might reflect that there is more to the ordinary blessings of our daily lives than meets the eye. Can we look beneath the surface of the good things we enjoy, such as food, clothes, warmth, friends, and see the hand of a loving Father at work? If, as the Psalm puts it, 'the heavens are telling the glory of God' (Ps 19:1), might not the daily, earthly – even earthy – blessings of our lives be telling us the same? Genuine faith does not demand miracles, but the eyes of faith will be quick to discern God's wonders, and lead us to respond with gratitude.

If we look through the Gospel, at the different reactions to which Jesus' miracles give rise, we can hardly escape the feeling that there is something rather ambivalent about the miracles. They do not prove faith. They can just as easily elicit a negative as a positive response from those who witness them. They certainly aren't intended to 'force' people into belief. There is always room for scepticism and doubt, even after a miracle. There will always be need for faith and trust, even after a miracle.

At times we believers may find ourselves longing for a miracle. Even if we do not express it so pointedly, there can be something within us that craves a final and complete confirmation of our faith in Christ. But at such times, we are a little like the Pharisees, demanding a sign (Mk 8:11). The Lord gives us enough to sustain our faith, but does not give us so much that our need for trust in him is lessened. If we try to see all of life's blessings as coming from his hand, we will have all the miracles we need.

148

Oratio

Repentance/resolve. Lord, the words 'Do you not care?' (Mk 4:38) are occasionally on our lips, as well as on the lips of your frightened apostles. Our slowness to perceive your blessings around us leads us at times to believe that you are not concerned for us, that you are allowing us sink in your very presence. We repent, Lord, of our lack of trust in you, of our slowness to see your wonders about us. Help us to look at life through the clear eye of faith, rather than the murky lens of fear and anxiety. May our concern for those around us help to work miracles for them of healing, of hope, of rescue from loneliness. 'There are many who say, "O that we might see some good! Let the light of your face shine on us O Lord!"' (Ps 4:6). May we see your goodness more clearly, and reflect your light to others!

Thanksgiving/praise. Perhaps the greatest miracle of all is our faith. We thank you, Lord, for the marvellous hope our faith holds out to us, and for the peace that only it can bring. We thank you for the people you have placed in our path at our times of greatest need: miracles themselves, who helped to rekindle the miracle of faith within us. With gratitude we renew our trust in you, as we pray: 'Our help is in the name of the Lord, who made heaven and earth' (Ps 124:8).

Intercession/petition. Continue to fill your people with hope, Lord, and with a sense of your gentle but powerful presence around us. Teach us to marvel not just at what is obviously 'marvellous,' but also at

149

the stream of more mundane blessings which we all too often take for granted. Your miracles, great and small, are an intimation that the whole world is indeed in your hands. May we grow in this conviction, and experience the deep trust that filled the heart of your Son asleep in the storm (Mk 4:38), and also the heart of the psalmist who prayed: 'I will both lie down and sleep in peace; for you alone, O Lord, make me lie down in safety' (Ps 4:8).

5. Following Jesus to the cross

Lectio. The cross is the centre of Mark's Gospel. It is anticipated almost from the beginning, and dominates the end. Jesus' whole ministry is carried out in the shadow of the cross. While miracles more or less dominate the first half of the Gospel, they give way to the cross in the latter half. Mark is letting us know that Jesus is not simply a wonder-worker: he is above all the suffering Messiah.

Two sections of Mark's Gospel are signed by the cross in a particular way. Obviously, the story of the passion of Jesus (ch. 14 and 15) is one of these. Not quite so obviously, but just as starkly, the cross overshadows the long section of Mark from 8:22 to 10:52.

Let us reflect for a moment on the cross. The fact that God's Son died on a cross is a shock and a scandal. In human terms, it is absurd. To human reasoning it is nonsense. To human eyes, it looks like a complete disaster. We cannot see any sense in it, unless we look at it through the eyes of faith. Our eyes need to be opened by faith if we are to see in the cross anything other than absurdity. Mark is acutely aware of the need for his readers' eyes to be opened in this sense, and this awareness determined how he composed the section of his Gospel from 8:22 to 10:52. Within this section of the Gospel, Jesus predicts his passion three times. This is a hard thing for his disciples to hear, and they both resist and misunderstand what he is saying. They are unable to *see* the sense of it.

For this reason, Mark begins and ends this section of his Gospel with acccunts of the healing of two blind people (8:22-26 and 10:46-52). What Jesus teaches in the intervening passages is the equivalent of opening the eyes of his disciples to the meaning of suffering: his own suffering as the Messiah, and the suffering which is part and parcel of discipleship. It took a miracle of healing for the two blind men to regain their sight, and it took a similar miracle for the eyes of the disciples to be opened to the meaning of suffering.

In Mark 8:27-30, Jesus asks his disciples who they think he is. It is not that Jesus has any doubts regarding his own identity. He is concerned rather with the identity of his disciples. The answer which his followers give to the question, 'Who do you say that I am?' determines *their* identity. If they accept that Jesus is the suffering Christ, then they, as his followers, will be able to accept suffering as a part of their identity. If they resist the notion of a suffering Messiah, they will remain scandalised and confused by suffering.

As soon as Peter confesses his faith in Jesus as the Messiah (8:29), Jesus begins to speak about the cross (8:31-33). Peter is left in no doubt that if he wishes to accept the authority and lordship of Jesus, he will also be confronted by the cross. Thinking back to our introduction to Mark and his reason for writing his Gospel, we can see that this will have been utterly relevant to the Christians for whom he wrote. These same Christians will also have been well able to identify with Peter's reaction to Jesus' prediction of his suffering and death (8:32): this must not happen! In spite of his faith in Jesus as the Christ (or perhaps because of it – Peter's faith was not yet mature), Peter is unwilling to accept that Jesus should suffer. Jesus' reaction to Peter's protest is harsh. He lets Peter know that his attitude is in complete contradiction to God's plan.

We might imagine that this episode would have been sufficient to convince the disciples of the place of the cross in Jesus' life, but it was not. Jesus makes two further predictions of his passion (9:30-32 and 10:32-34). On each occasion, it becomes immediately clear that the disciples do not have any grasp of the real meaning of Jesus' words. Just after Jesus second prediction of his passion, they argue about which of them is the greatest (9:33-37). Following the third prediction, two of the disciples approach Jesus to ask for preferential treatment in the new kingdom which he is establishing, and this provokes great resentment among the others (10:35-45). Clearly, Jesus' followers are simply not on his wavelength. They seem incapable of accepting what he is trying to teach them. In a word, their eyes are closed.

Take some time to read through the section of Mark we have been looking at (8:22-10:52). As you do so, notice that there are several indicators of a steady movement by Jesus and his followers (8:22,

27; 9:30; 10:1, 17, 32, 46, 52). They are not staying in one place, but travelling. They are not wandering, but moving steadily (if indirectly) towards a destination. This destination is Jerusalem, and the cross. It is *along the way*, as they follow Jesus, that the disciples begin to learn about the cross. Here they begin to discover – however much they resist the idea – that the way of Jesus is the way of the cross, and that to follow him means to follow him to the cross.

The people for whom Mark wrote his Gospel were making the painful discovery that the cross was to have a prominent place in *their* lives. Movement toward it was inevitable if they were following Jesus. Jesus would not be deflected. Instead, he would deflect his followers from their petty concerns and ambitions, and teach them that the cross was central to his way of suffering, sacrificial love. It is in keeping with this theme of the centrality of the cross in discipleship that this part of Mark's Gospel also contains some of Jesus' most demanding teachings, such as the need for renunciation of oneself (9:35), the forbidding of divorce (10:1-12) and the danger of riches (10:17-27).

We have seen that Jesus has a number of titles in Mark's Gospel. He is the Christ (the Messiah), Son of God, King. There is a further title which is used only by Jesus himself, and that is 'Son of Man'. This title has its roots in the Old Testament, and Jesus uses it when he is referring to his own sufferings, including each of his three predictions of his passion (see 8:31; 9:9, 12, 31; 10:33, 45; 14:21, 41). 'Son of Man' is the title of the suffering Jesus. Whatever titles others may confer on him (including Peter's sincere but ignorant acknowledgement that he is the Christ), Jesus' favourite title for himself is 'Son of Man'. Jesus identifies himself above all as the one who freely undergoes great suffering out of love for humanity.

Meditatio

We can see much of ourselves reflected in the disciples, as they struggle with – and against – Jesus' single-minded determination to endure suffering. Their confusion and resistance is a source of consolation to us, when we find ourselves in the same position. The disciples were far from perfect (as we shall soon see in greater detail); their understanding was very limited. But Jesus did not require perfection of them, and gently nursed them along, as they slowly came to grips with the knowledge that he was not even going to attempt to avoid the cross.

The avoidance of suffering is written into us as a law of our human nature. This is a very good thing! Discipleship is not, nor should it be, a pursuit of suffering. But integrity will inevitably, at times, cause us to suffer, and the total integrity of Jesus caused him to suffer in a terrible way. We are called neither to pursue suffering, nor to flee it when it is the price of our integrity as the followers of Jesus.

Perhaps we can recall a moment when we reacted to the suffering of a loved one in the way that Peter reacted to Jesus' first prediction of his passion. In our desire to spare those we care about from suffering, have we ever attempted to deflect them from pursuing what they knew to be right? 'Don't get involved – it's not worth it'... addressed to a faithful disciple, such sentiments can be the exact opposite to the attitude of Jesus. They can be the voice of temptation, however sincerely intended.

Again, we might have to admit blindness to the crosses borne by those around us. Someone close to us may have been bearing a heavy burden, and we, like the disciples, remained tied up in our own petty concerns and projects, desensitised by self-concern. The healing of our blindness entails healing from ambition and attachment to comfort, and from the sort of false concern – for ourselves and for others – that would attach ultimate priority not to the will of God, but to the easier option.

Central to the process of maturing as a Christian disciple is coming to understand that suffering is not an unmitigated disaster, to be avoided at all costs. Rather, it is something which can tap into what is most noble within us; something which can raise us to a new, ultimately more human level of existence. The suffering of Jesus is not, after all, the lowest point, but the glorious highpoint of his ministry. In the Gospel of John, just as in Mark's Gospel, Jesus makes three predictions of his passion, but each time he refers to it as his exaltation (Jn 3:13-14; 8:28; 12:32). When Jesus is raised up on the cross, he is raised as a king, victorious over all suffering, even death itself. The journey of discipleship involves learning to see the cross not as a defeat but as a victory; learning the mindset of St Paul, who wrote: 'May I never boast of anything except the cross of our Lord Jesus Christ' (Gal 6:14).

All of this is a slow process indeed. Through the ministry of Jesus, the blind man at Bethsaida recovered his sight not instantaneously but gradually, in stages. For us, the opening of the eyes of faith is an ongoing, lifelong process. When the blind man on the road to Jericho received his sight, his reaction was the one to which all disciples are called: he followed Jesus on the way (10:52). This is the way to Jerusalem, along which Jesus teaches us and questions us. If we remain faithful to the struggle to answer the question, 'Who do you say that I am?' (Mk 8:29), the Lord will gradually lead us to full sight, and to a deep appreciation of the place and value of the cross in our lives.

Oratio

Repentance/resolve. There is none so blind as the one who will not see! We repent, Lord, of any unwillingness we have felt to see your loving hand in the sufferings which you permit us, or our loved ones, to experience. We repent also of our lack of sensitivity to those in our midst who carry heavy crosses. Give us compassionate hearts and helping hands. May we take to ourselves the words which you spoke to the disciples on the road to Emmaus: 'How foolish you are, and how slow of heart to believe all that the prophets have declared! Was it not necessary that the Messiah should suffer these things and then enter into his glory?' (Lk 24:25-26).

Thanksgiving/praise. We thank you Lord for suffering for us. What led you to the cross, what kept you on the cross in the face of those who taunted you, telling you to save yourself (Mk 15:30), was your love for us. We thank you yet again for the tremendous hope which your cross holds out to us: the hope – the certainty – that every suffering you permit your people to endure has a meaning and a value. What died on the cross was despair, and so we, your people, can pray with confidence: 'You have kept count of my tossings; put my tears in your bottle... This I know, that God is for me. In God, whose word I praise, in the Lord, whose word I praise, in God I trust; I am not afraid' (Ps 56:8-10).

Intercession/petition. Lord, grant us to persevere in following you along the way, even when our vision is not clear, when we cannot see further than Calvary. Give us a sincere desire to help others bear their burdens. Give us words of hope and encouragement for them. Give us sensitivity, strength and compassion, as we walk together with them on the way of the cross. Once again, may we learn from your apostle Paul, who teaches us: 'Bear one another's burdens, and in this way you will fulfil the law of Christ' (Gal 6:2).

6. Jesus' weak disciples

Lectio. By now, we have an impression of the 'form' of the disciples. It is clear that they are, to say the very least, rather dense and lacklustre. Mark, in fact, portrays them as deteriorating as the story unfolds. At first, they have simply no idea of the identity or power of Jesus, and lack even the most elementary faith in him ('Have you still no faith?', 4:40). They are no better at the very end of the Gospel, and refuse to believe the news of the resurrection, even when they are told a second time, 16:11, 13). They are terrified during a storm, even though Jesus is with them, and uncomprehending when he calms the sea (4:35-41). Despite witnessing his great power on this occasion, they are 'utterly astounded' at the second miracle involving the sea (6:47-52). After witnessing the two miracles of the loaves, they still fret about not having enough food with them (8:14-21).

When they finally come to the realisation that Jesus is the Messiah (8:27-30), the disciples continue to think only in terms of their own prestige (9:33-37; 10:35-45). When the time of Jesus' passion arrives, they desert him completely (14:50). Peter, their leader, perseveres with Jesus for another few hours, but only to let him down in a still more pitiful manner (14:66-72).

In addition to their failures in courage and trust, Mark reveals a small-mindedness and pettiness in the disciples. They fail not only as followers of Jesus, but as human beings. They yield not only where there is pressure, but also where there is none. They are failed exorcists (9:18) who begrudge success to anyone else (9:38-40). They try to prevent access to their Master by those whom they consider to be insignificant (10:13-16). They have a more than ample share of ambition, with its attendant resentfulness (10:35-45).

Mark's audience, faced with opposition and persecution on account of their fidelity to Christ, will have taken comfort from the weakness of Jesus' earliest followers. Mark shows them – and us – that Jesus sticks with his inept friends, even when they desert him. They are his first concern after the resurrection (16:7). To them, in spite of all their failures, he entrusts the task of preaching the Good

News to the whole world (16:15). The misery of the apostles and the mercy of Jesus encourage all those who encounter Mark's Good News to lean on the grace of God rather than on any strength or virtue of their own. The words of Jesus in Mark 2:17, 'I have come to call not the righteous but sinners,' apply not only to pagans and the outcast, but just as much to those who are closest to Jesus.

Meditatio

Once again, Mark's portrayal of the disciples invites and challenges us to examine ourselves. We are not much different to them. We have the same fears, the same pride. Like them, we can vacillate between despair on the one hand and arrogance on the other. We can feel filled with faith and hope one day, only to feel utterly dejected the next – perhaps after a minor setback, perhaps simply on account of our mood. These words of the psalmist might have been written with us in mind: 'As for me, I said in my prosperity, "I shall never be moved." By your favour, O Lord, you had established me as a strong mountain; you hid your face; I was dismayed' (Ps 30:6-7).

Insofar as we might ever feel filled with faith, we will actually be running ahead of the disciples as Mark portrays them. Jesus' question to them, 'Have you still no faith?', resounds through the entire Gospel. We might find some more of our faith-experience reflected a little further afield, in the Gospel of Matthew, where we see a slight improvement in how the disciples' faith is portrayed. In Matthew, Jesus addresses his disciples as 'You of little faith' (Mt 6:30; 8:26; 14:31; 16:8). Not much faith is required of them – if their faith is the size of a mustard seed, they will move mountains (Mt 17:20), but at times their faith seems so tiny that only the Lord himself could discern it! Perhaps we can resonate with this experience also. Even when we are most sorely tried, even if we are bitter with God, we still have some little faith. This seed of faith does not give us an easy passage through life's storms, but it can whisper some hope to us when we are most in need.

In the Gospel of Luke, the faith of the disciples is portrayed in yet a different light. Unlike the dithering disciples we meet in Mark's Gospel, those we meet in Luke run the risk of over-confidence. They seem to have, if anything, too much faith! We see this in James and John, who appear to believe that as Jesus' disciples they can call fire from heaven on those who refuse to show hospitality to Jesus (Lk 9:51-56). Again, we see it at the return of the seventy disciples from their first mission trip (Lk 10:17-20). They are filled with delight over the power which they have exercised in the name of Jesus, but Jesus dampens down their enthusiasm, reminding them that what they should delight most in is not any power they have been given, but the promise of salvation which is theirs. We can identify with the exuberance of Luke's disciples. Our good moments can feel very good indeed, but we need to guard our hearts from pride, and remember that it is by the grace of God that we live, and not by our own merit.

The first three Gospels, then, provide very different pictures of the faith experience of Jesus' earliest followers.[6] At any given time, we may find our own situation reflected clearly in one or other of these portraits. One thing they have in common (but which is most clearly expressed in Mark) is that they present the heart of discipleship as a trustful dependence on Jesus, rather than trust in oneself and one's own strength and virtue. In this, the Gospels tell us, like Saint Paul, that 'since all have sinned and fall short of the glory of God; they are now justified by his grace as a gift, through the redemption that is in Christ Jesus' (Rom 3:23-24). Mark above all, in his unflinchingly frank portrayal of the earliest followers of Jesus, reminds all subsequent disciples that 'God proves his love for us in that while we still were sinners Christ died for us' (Rom 5:8).

Oratio

Repentance/resolve. We repent, Lord, of our preoccupation with ourselves. Too often, we are like the rich fool (Lk 12:16-21), anxious to fill our lives and our egos with what is not of you. Help us to find joy and enthusiasm not in our pet projects, but in serving you as you wish to be served. Forgive our slowness to act. We have been content to gather new insights – even the very best of insights – into faith and discipleship, but unless we let these take flesh within us, they are not faith, but remain inane and futile. Help us so to live that we can sing with the psalmist: 'You have delivered my soul from death, and my feet from falling, so that I may walk before God in the light of life' (Ps 56:13).

Thanksgiving/praise. We thank you, merciful and compassionate Saviour, for sticking with us even when we have not stuck with you! We thank you for your tolerance of our slowness, and for your slowness to condemn us. May we reflect these wonderful qualities to others, and with them learn to pray: 'It is good to give thanks to the Lord, to sing praises to your name, O Most High; to declare your steadfast love in the morning, and your faithfulness by night' (Ps 92:1-2).

Intercession/petition. Look with kindness, Lord, on those whose faith is weak, on those who have lost their faith, and on those who have never had faith in you. Lead all your people away from reliance on their own strength, even as they labour to bring about your kingdom. May we place our trust only in you – not as a substitute for action, or as an excuse for complacency, but because we believe that it is only in you that our best efforts will bear fruit. 'Not to us, O Lord, not to us, but to your name give glory' (Ps 115:1).

7. Facing Resistance

Lectio. We have already seen that Mark wanted to draw a parallel between the suffering of the disciples (both the disciples in the Gospel and later disciples) and those of Jesus. While only the sufferings of Jesus, as Messiah and Son of God, could have brought salvation, the sufferings his disciples undergo have great value when they are seen, in faith, as a participation in the sufferings of Jesus himself. We have seen also that Jesus encountered resistance from the very beginning of his ministry, and Mark would like his audience to know that they can expect the same, if they choose to be faithful to Jesus.

In what way might the resistance met by Jesus be paralleled in the lives of his followers? To answer this, let us look at the kind of resistance Jesus actually meets as he moves, preaching and healing, through Galilee and gradually onward towards Jerusalem. Overall, Jesus meets resistance from three sources. First of all, he has to contend with resistance from the authorities of the world in which he moves. The religious authorities – named by Mark as the Pharisees and scribes – are deeply disturbed by what Jesus says and does. They see him as a dangerous liberal, flouting their holiest laws in a way that gives rise to great scandal. Among the habits of Jesus which they find particularly galling are his practice of eating with known sinners (2:16), his apparent disregard for the holiness of the Sabbath (3:2), and his carelessness regarding ritual cleanness and uncleanness (7:1-13).

Because of the perceived political implications of Jesus' actions (his challenging of details of the status quo could, if he gained enough followers, have broader implications for the social order), the religious powers are joined in their opposition to Jesus by the secular powers. Mark introduces these early in the Gospel (3:6), in his mention of the Herodians, a group associated with the dynasty to which Herod, the Roman-sponsored ruler of Galilee, belonged. Mark presents the religious and secular powers as partners in crime, plotting together to destroy Jesus.[7]

The second source of resistance to Jesus is not in his enemies, but in his friends. He has to struggle with their weakness on a range of fronts. Their incomprehension, slowness, misguided concern, ambition, pettiness, resentment and fear add to the burden of opposition which Jesus already faces from his enemies. Betrayal by Judas and denial by Peter increase his isolation and pain. With the exception of Judas, whose treachery is deliberate, the apostles are not bad individuals. Their intentions are good, but they are often betrayed by their weakness. As Jesus tells them in the garden of Gethsemane: 'The spirit indeed is willing, but the flesh is weak' (Mk 14:38).

It is in the spiritual powers of evil that Jesus encounters the most sustained and vicious opposition. Whereas his disciples and the powers of the world are objects of his concern, Jesus is in direct and open confrontation with the powers of evil. He throws down the gauntlet from the very beginning, and the first healing he works is an exorcism (1:23-28). The evil spirits know precisely who he is, and confess his identity clearly (5:7). Such confession lets us know that while Jesus' human opponents may be misguided or weak, his spiritual enemies are fully aware of what they are doing, and therefore irreversibly hardened in their choice of evil. These spiritual enemies of Jesus also orchestrate the human opposition to him, a point which John brings out clearly in his Gospel, when he tells us that 'the devil had already put it into the heart of Judas son of Simon Iscariot to betray him' (Jn 13:2).

Meditatio

Christian tradition has always been aware of the parallel between the resistance faced by Jesus during his life and that which his followers may have to face. This tradition refers to three great areas of struggle and temptation for the believer: the world, the flesh and the devil. The followers of Jesus do battle on these three fronts, just as Jesus himself had done. Of course, discipleship is not a constant battle, and not everyone will be faced with the type of resistance we read about in Mark, but every believer will at times need to struggle 'like a good soldier of Christ Jesus' (2 Tim 2:3).

Some older approaches to spirituality may have tended to be rather preoccupied with the snares and temptations of the world. But as Christians we are not called to 'play safe,' to have the minimum contact necessary with 'worldly' affairs. We are instead called to be fully engaged with the society in which we live, to transform it from the inside, rather than look on fearfully or disdainfully from a safe distance. Of course we are also asked to be prudent, and to take reasonable care to guard our hearts and minds from temptation. Traditional spirituality speaks of the need to avoid what it calls 'occasions of sin'. Underlying this is a very sound insight, which wisely recognises that remaining free from sin often has more to do with the absence of opportunity than the presence of virtue.

Many if not most people, when they hear the word 'flesh' used in the context of Christian spirituality or morality, presume automatically that sexual sin or temptation is being referred to. But the word 'flesh' has a much broader meaning: it refers to weak, fallen human nature as a whole. To struggle with the resistance offered by the flesh is to struggle with a kind of spiritual or moral gravitational force. When the disciples fell asleep during the hour of Jesus' agony, they did not choose to leave him alone and isolated, they were overcome – pulled down – by their own weakness. When, for example, we struggle with resentment or impatience, we resist a natural, instinctive pull which we experience within ourselves.

The Lord provides us with ample 'resistance training' in our struggles with 'flesh'. What might be considered a classic example of such 'training' is in the area of patience. It is not uncommon to hear people remark, with some surprise, that after they prayed for greater patience, they began to feel that they had become *less* patient. What may have happened is that the answer to their prayer took the form of a series of opportunities to practice patience and grow in it. And every opportunity to practice patience is also – potentially – an occasion of impatience! Conversely, every struggle with the 'flesh', with our fallen human nature, can be an opportunity for growth. Ironically, the Lord can bless us even by allowing us to be tempted.

It would be most unhealthy for Christians to attribute directly to the devil every single resistance they feel in their efforts to live out the Gospel. In practice, our human weakness can make temptation practically redundant, and it might be more honest to recognise this, than to point habitually to an external cause for our failures. However, the Gospel of Mark and many other biblical texts make it clear that spiritual evil is a reality. If, as the Second Letter to Timothy puts it, to be a believer is to be a 'soldier of Christ Jesus', we would be very poor soldiers indeed, were we to fail to recognise the enemy – or even deny his existence! While keeping a healthy balance, we should also bear in mind the words of St Paul in his Letter to the Ephesians: 'Our struggle is not against enemies of blood and flesh, but against the rulers, against the authorities, against the cosmic powers of this present darkness, against the spiritual forces of evil in the heavenly places' (6:12). The key to victory in this and all other struggles is not our own strength, but our obedience to the will of God, after the pattern of Jesus himself, in the hour of his most intense struggle (Mk 14:36).

Oratio

Repentance/resolve. Forgive us, Lord, for those times when our failings have sprung not so much from weakness as from laziness, when we have made no real effort, when we have ignored your promise to be with us, and have not turned to you for strength. We resolve to 'fight the good fight' (1 Tim 6:12), on all fronts, with renewed confidence in the promise you have made to us through your servant Paul: 'God is faithful, and he will not let you be tested beyond your strength, but with the testing he will also provide the way out so that you may be able to endure it' (1 Cor 10:13).

Thanksgiving/praise. We thank you for the wisdom you give us in your word, which is not simply information, but is 'living and active' (Heb 4:12). We thank you also for your promise to your people when they were being threatened by the Egyptians, a promise we claim for ourselves: 'The Lord will fight for you, and you have only to keep still' (Ex 14:14). We accept this word not in a spirit of complacency, but in a spirit of active trust in you. May we find our strength in you, and so share the prayer of Moses and your people: 'The Lord is my strength and my might, and he has become my salvation; this is my God, and I will praise him' (Ex 15:2).

Intercession/petition. We pray to you, Lord, as you have taught us to pray, that we may not be put to the test (Mk 14:38; Mt 6:13). Help us to be watchful and alert. We pray for those whose strength is failing, those who are tempted to give up the struggle. May all your people come to know your power, and experience the confidence which led St Paul to proclaim: 'I toil and struggle with all the energy that he powerfully inspires within me' (Col 1:29).

8. Images that challenge

Lectio. Much of Jesus' teaching in the Gospels takes the form of parables. Every believer is well acquainted with the better-known parables, such as the parable of the prodigal son, in Luke's Gospel, which we looked at earlier. Mark has fewer parables than Luke (or Matthew), but they are still an important part of his Gospel. What exactly is a parable? In the Gospels, the word 'parable' can refer to sayings, proverbs, comparisons, metaphors, stories or allegories (extended comparisons). What all of these different forms have in common is that they are *illustrations* of what Jesus wishes to teach. They take scenes or objects from ordinary daily life (clothes, meals, plants, light, relationships…), and use them as images for what is beyond the ordinary. The parables are like verbal

Trojan horses, apparently benign, but once we take them in, they can have an unsettling and transforming effect. In his parables, Jesus occasionally takes advantage of the power of story; and he always takes advantage of the humdrum and ordinary as an unsuspected way of planting a powerful message in the minds of his hearers.

When he tells a parable, Jesus invariably *challenges* his audience, confronting them with the nature and values of the kingdom which he is preaching. However, Jesus himself seems to say quite the opposite in Mark 4:10-12, where he tells his disciples that he uses parables not as illustrations calling people to conversion, but in order to hide things from people, so that they might *not* convert! The best way to understand this rather odd passage is probably to see it as a description of the effect of parables on people who have simply no interest in being converted. Those who are 'outside', who listen to Jesus only as critics, in confrontation with him, will not be lead to honest self-criticism when they hear Jesus' parables. They will only be hardened further in their resistance to Jesus. This is clear in Mark 12:12, where the religious authorities are angered by a parable Jesus tells, because 'they realised that he had told this parable against them.' As *challenging images*, the parables can speak 'against' all those who hear them. Some people rise to the challenge, others resent it.

The parable of the sower (Mk 4:1-9) is exceptional, in that it is the only parable followed by a detailed explanation (Mk 4:13-20). It is in fact the most important of the parables. It is the key to the rest, as Jesus makes clear when he asks the twelve,

'Do you not understand this parable? Then how will you understand all the parables?' (4:13). The fundamental concern of every parable is that Jesus' word take root in his hearers. This concern is sometimes hidden and implicit, but it is the explicit concern of the parable of the sower. This parable interrogates its hearers loudly and clearly: 'Which type of ground are you?' 'How are you receiving the word?'

In this parable and his explanation of it, Jesus teaches not just the obvious fact that some people receive the word well and others badly; he reflects on *why* some receive it badly and on the obstacles to receiving it well. Those who fail to yield fruit have succumbed to the kinds of resistance we described earlier: resistance from the world, its powers and priorities (4:17); from the flesh – weak, ambitious or anxious human nature (4:19); and from the devil (4:15). In this parable and Jesus' explanation of it, we have a whole spirituality of the word and our hearing of it.

Meditatio

Read Mark 4:1-20. How many times do you meet the word 'listen' or 'hear'?[8] If we listen carefully to this parable, it can reveal to us the quality of our listening to the word of God as a whole. It is a parable about receiving the word and putting it into practice – it is a parable about *lectio divina*. Which of the four kinds of ground in verses 4-8 do we most identify with? The mere fact that we are considering the question makes it unlikely that we are the path where the word has no effect at all, but is taken away immediately by Satan (although we might have to admit that we are capable of great carelessness in how we receive the word). This leaves three further options.

We may be among those who receive the word with sincere goodwill, even joyful enthusiasm, but who do not have staying-power. While a 'respectable' religion can be built on vague feelings of goodwill, a life-transforming faith needs to be rooted in God's word, and this is what is missing from those who received the word in rocky ground. The followers of Jesus will be known not by their exuberance, but by their fruits (Mt 7:20).

The problem with those who receive God's word like seed falling among thorns is not so much a lack of rootedness as an abundance of other concerns which crowd out the word. We can make some space in our lives for God and his word – a tidy compartment, under our control. But the kingdom of God is a very vigorous plant (Mk 4:30-32), and its roots need to fill not a corner of our lives, but all the space we have. If we try to section off our faith and our hearing of God's word, we will choke the development of the kingdom of God in our lives. It will simply not compete with all the other concerns we have. The word of God grows and bears fruit in the lives of those for whom it is the number one priority.

It is human nature to be aware of one's failings, and we may hesitate to see ourselves as the good soil, receiving God's word in a way that brings a harvest of transformation. But the parable of the sower ends on a very hopeful note. There are degrees of receptiveness. Those who receive the word in good soil may yield thirty, or sixty, or a hundredfold. While we may not wish to claim the highest success, we can see where the word has borne *some* fruit in our lives, and this gives us encouragement and hope. We need not think in black and white terms of total success and total failure: we can rejoice in modest fruits, in small fidelities to the word of God.

While our first contact with the parable of the sower invites us to ask ourselves which type of soil we are, sustained reflection on it will show us that we are in fact a mixed field, a blend of fidelity and infidelity. In this, like all the parables, the parable of the sower challenges us not only to identify where we are, but to move on from there to a fuller response to God.

Oratio

Repentance/resolve. How often we have played with your word, Lord. Your word can be touching, fascinating, intriguing – but above all you intend it to be transforming. Forgive us for approaching it more as a work of art or curiosity than as a seed of enormous potential which you wish to plant within us. Forgive us for approaching it as one other interest among many, for choking it by our superficiality. May your word take root in us so that we may be 'doers of the word, and not merely hearers who deceive themselves' (Jas 1:22).

Thanksgiving/praise. 'What does the Lord require of you but to do justice, and to love kindness, and to walk humbly with your God?' (Mic 6:8). We thank you, Lord, for speaking to us, for showing us your will, for the light and guidance your word gives to our lives. 'Surely, this commandment that I am commanding you today is not too hard for you, nor is it too far away… No, the word is very near to you; it is in your mouth and in your heart for you to observe (Deut 30:11, 14). Thank you, Lord God, for drawing close and speaking plainly to us. In all the circumstances of our lives, your word is 'a word in season, how good it is!' (Prov 15:23).

Intercession/petition. Lord, someone has defined faith as leaning on your word so heavily that if it were removed we would fall over. Lead us to do this; to open our hearts to your word, so that being fertile soil, we might build our lives on the rock of wisdom which is given to those who are hearers and doers of your word (Mt 7:24). May we become more radical disciples, more deeply rooted in your word. May we come to know deeply that 'one does not live by bread alone, but by every word that comes from the mouth of God' (Mt 4:4).

9. The suffering Messiah revealed

Lectio. Mark's whole Gospel converges on the passion of Jesus. The bitter opposition he had to face is signalled from near the beginning. Jesus' whole movement – and that of his closest followers – is a gradual journey towards the cross. The story of the passion, from the plotting of the authorities and the anointing of Jesus in Bethany, through to his burial, takes up chapters 14 and 15 of Mark's Gospel. Before continuing, it would be well to take time to read these two chapters carefully.

The passion is above all the moment when Jesus

can afford to reveal his identity fully (14:62). Now, there is simply no chance of anyone misunderstanding him: he is not about to take the world by storm, to seek status for himself or offer it to his followers, or to overwhelm people with a demonstration of divine power. His way is the way of weakness – of crucified love.

We have said that a library could be filled with writings on the Gospel of Mark, and this could almost be said of writings on the passion story alone. We will have to limit ourselves to just a few aspects of the story – hopefully enough to give us a sense of Mark's main concerns as he follows the progress of Jesus to the cross.

A theme which runs through the passion is the increasing loneliness and isolation of Jesus. In the garden of Gethsemane, he suffers the kind of painful isolation which can be experienced by those who are in the company of others, yet feel no sense of connection with them. His disciples are physically present, but of no support whatever, as they sleep through the trauma their friend is enduring. A short time later, they flee altogether, as they sense the real danger which surrounds Jesus. Peter's denial (14:66-72) is not just an impulse. He has the opportunity to make up for what might have been an initial moment of weakness, but his second and third denials are even more emphatic. At this moment of fear and tension, he sees his friendship with Jesus only as a liability.

As the story continues, Jesus' isolation deepens still further. There is an infinite distance between him and the crowd who demand his execution (15:6-15). He is mocked by his Roman guards (15:16-20). The mocking continues even after he is finally crucified, and those who are crucified with him taunt him also (15:32). But Jesus' isolation is not complete. He is the Son of God, he can trust in his Father, to whom he has prayed: 'Not what I want, but what you want' (14:36). Surely, God will take care of his obedient Son? As he weakens on the cross, however, Jesus reaches a point of total despair, and the conviction that he has been abandoned by God leads him to cry out: 'My God, my God, why have you forsaken me?' (15:34).[9]

At this point, there is nothing more to suffer. Jesus' isolation and pain are total: there is nobody left to reject him! He has drunk the cup of suffering dry (Mk 10:39), and now dies with a cry of anguish on his lips (15:37). Earlier, we saw that crucifixion was *the* death for sinners, those who were cursed by God. We have also seen, while reflecting on the call of Abraham, that the consequence of sin is a loss of solidarity with God and others. This is precisely what the crucified Jesus experiences: a devastating loneliness and lack of solidarity, first with others, then even with God himself. Jesus experiences, in his own person, the full consequences of sin. In a sense, he *becomes* sin. At the time of his baptism, Jesus identified himself with sinners, lining up to receive John's baptism of repentance in the river Jordan. Now he bears the burden of sin, and its terrible consequences. He does this so that those who believe in him might be spared these consequences, and shows us that indeed 'the Son of Man came not to be served but to serve, and to give his life a ransom for many' (Mk 10:45).

The meaning of Jesus' words at the last supper (Mk 14:22-25) becomes clear at the time of his death. At his last meal with his disciples, Jesus offers his flesh and blood to them, telling them that his blood is 'the blood of the covenant, which is poured out for many' (Mk 14:24). Up to now, the 'blood of the covenant' has been the blood of animals: blood sprinkled on the people gathered at Mount Sinai, to seal the covenant which God had made with them (Ex 24:8); the blood of bulls and goats sprinkled in the holiest part of the Temple on the yearly feast of Atonement.

At the last supper, closest to Jesus' mind will have been the blood of the lamb, sprinkled on the Israelites' door-posts on the night of their escape from Egypt. This was a signal to the angel sent to kill the firstborn of the Egyptians, telling him to *pass over* their homes without harming them (Ex 12:21-27). The meal which Jesus shares with his disciples is a *Passover* meal (Mk 14:12-16), the highpoint of the annual feast commemorating the exodus, when God freed his people from slavery in Egypt. Now God is freeing his people from slavery to sin, and it is the blood of Jesus, shed on the cross, which will cause the anger of God to pass over them. No longer will people be asked to sacrifice a lamb at Passover time, because Christ has offered the permanent and totally effective sacrifice of his own self: 'Our paschal lamb, Christ, has been sacrificed' (1 Cor 5:7).

Mark very concretely underlines the reality of Jesus' death for sinners by recounting the incident involving Barabbas (Mk 15:6-15). Barabbas is a murderer, probably a politically motivated one – a terrorist. Under pressure from the crowds, Pilate decides to release him and execute Jesus: justice is perverted, and guilt swaps places with innocence. From the perspective of Jesus' enemies, the guilty one must go free so that the innocent one could die. From a divine perspective, the innocent one is condemned to die so that the guilty might go free. The mystery at the heart of the passion is that God uses the most terrible sin of all to rescue people from sin.

There are many other players in the terrible drama of the passion – 'drama' being an apt word, since Mark recounts events more as would a dramatist than a reporter. He is concerned not so much to present a blow-by-blow account of events, as to involve his audience, inviting them to enter into the plot, asking themselves where they stand, and with whom. Mark's account of the passion is therefore truly an invitation to *lectio divina*.

In his description of the disciples in Gethsemane, Mark invites his audience to reflect on their commitment and alertness. Gethsemane is the last occasion in Mark's Gospel when we see Jesus and his disciples together. It is also the time when Jesus most needs the company of his disciples. If this is a test, the disciples fail it miserably by falling asleep. Mark's description of Peter in the courtyard of the high priest invites his audience to reflect on their courage. Will they, like Peter, submit fearfully to the cynicism of others? If they have already done so, will they at least recover their integrity and, again like Peter, 'break down and weep' (Mk 14:72)? In his description of Pilate, more concerned to appease the crowd than to see justice done, Mark appeals to the integrity of his audience. Their faith in Jesus demands choices, sometimes very difficult ones. If they try to avoid choosing, and – like Pilate – sit on the fence, they will choose badly by default.

Particularly significant in Mark's story of the passion are those who mock Jesus. This applies not so much to the mocking soldiers (15:16-20), whose mockery of unfortunate prisoners might have been a matter of routine, as to those who mock Jesus while he is on the cross (15:25-32). In demanding that Jesus rescue himself miraculously so that they might believe, these people pervert the nature of faith. True faith is trustful submission to God. It can give rise to miracles, but never demands them as a pre-condition. The mockers at the cross glibly announce that if they see a miracle they will believe. They have none of that authentic faith which sees *because* it believes. Their demand for a miracle also ignores the close connection between faith and repentance, a connection made by Jesus in his very first words in the Gospel: 'Repent, and believe' (1:15).

Ironically, the mockers are quite right when they say about Jesus: 'He cannot save himself' (15:31). The truth is that Jesus cannot save himself and at the same time be obedient to the saving will of his Father. In Jesus, the mockers see only powerlessness, and refuse to believe. As they see it, remaining on the cross is totally inconsistent with being the Messiah and Saviour of Israel. Jesus himself knows that this is the only way that he *can* be Messiah and Saviour. It is Mark's hope that those who read his Gospel will come to realise this also, and that having learned it, they will not be so scandalised by what they themselves suffer as followers of the one who exercised infinite power in his obedient weakness on the cross.

Meditatio

We, the readers of Mark, know that the story of Jesus ends with the resurrection. This implicitly guides our whole reading of the Gospel. We are somewhat like children reading a tale of mystery and suspense, who know that the ending will be a happy one. The Gospel of Mark was written in the light of Easter faith, and the entire life of Jesus is understood in this light. Mark wrote his Gospel to show us that everything that preceded the resurrection was part of God's plan. There is no inconsistency between belief in the resurrection and suffering in the lives of those who believe. The miracle which faith accepts is that God drew the greatest good from the most terrible evil. Therefore the story of Jesus' passion holds out hope to all who suffer. This is why, in spite of its unblinking focus on the suffering of Jesus and the weakness of his followers, Mark's Gospel is a story of incredible hope. Those who have faith in Jesus claim for themselves the hope described in the latest book of the Old Testament, written just a few decades before the birth of Jesus: 'The souls of the righteous are in the hands of God, and no torment will ever touch them. In the eyes of the foolish they seemed to have died, and their departure was thought to be a disaster, and their going from us to be their destruction; but they are at peace. For though in the sight of others they were punished, their hope is full of immortality' (Wis 3:1-4).

If, overall, Mark's Gospel shows us that discipleship is not for the strong or the perfect, his telling of the passion story drives home the point. Peter, the leader of the disciples, the one whom Jesus – perhaps not without a touch of irony – nicknamed 'the rock', proves to be among the weakest of Jesus' followers. All of Jesus' closest followers prove very fragile indeed. Where did Mark get so much negative information on these earliest followers of Jesus? Undoubtedly, the information Mark wove into his account originated with the disciples themselves. They made no attempt to play down their poor performance, but saw that their weakness could itself be part of the good news. Rather than hiding their failures, the disciples broadcast them for all to hear. Their confession of failure was a *confessio laudis*, a confession of praise of the great mercy of the Lord who did not give up on them. If the Lord could work with such poor material, then there could only be hope for all those who would subsequently struggle to follow Jesus. The Gospel invites us not to be discouraged by weakness and failure, but to entrust ourselves repeatedly and confidently to God's mercy.

We should reflect at length on the question asked by those who mocked the crucified Jesus, for it is our question too. Why does Jesus remain inactive in the face of suffering? Why does the one who healed so often during his life remain silent, and apparently absent, when his latter-day followers suffer? While Jesus' mockers maintained that they would begin to believe if they saw him act, many of those who follow Jesus fear that unless they see him act, they will cease to believe. The Gospel makes no attempt to give us an intellectual answer to this painful mystery. It simply invites us to contemplate the crucified Christ, and so to grow in the trust that our faith will eventually lead us to see things clearly.

Oratio

Repentance/resolve. Lord, we have not taken your love – for ourselves and for others – seriously enough. May we never take our sinfulness more seriously than we take your mercy, but trust in the words we read in the First Letter of Peter: 'The God of all grace, who has called you to his eternal glory in Christ, will himself restore, support, strengthen, and establish you' (5:10). May we in our turn reflect in all our dealings with others the marvellous love of Christ, who 'suffered for us, leaving us an example, so that we should follow in his steps' (cf. 1 Peter 2:21).

Thanksgiving/praise. 'What shall I return to the Lord for all his bounty to me?' (Ps 116:12). There are no words adequate to express the gratitude that we should feel for your love, O Lord. With humble gratitude, we offer you the words of the Church's great Easter hymn, the *Exsultet*: 'Father, how wonderful your care for us! How boundless your merciful love! To ransom a slave you gave away your Son. O happy fault, O necessary sin of Adam, which gained for us so great a Redeemer!'

Intercession/petition. We raise up to you, Lord, all those who drink a cup of sorrow and pain, those who despair at their own weakness. Give us hearts sensitive to those who share the 'bread of adversity and the water of affliction' (Is 30:20). May they, with our help, come to share in the tested faith of Job, and pray confidently with him: 'I know that my Redeemer lives' (Job 19:25).

10. Empty tomb – new beginning

Lectio. 'On the third day he rose again.' This is the creed of all Christians. By our modern way of reckoning time, we would say that the body of Jesus lay in the tomb for two days: from Friday to Sunday, having lain there for the full duration of the Sabbath. In Jesus' time, this was reckoned as three days, since the day on which he was placed in the tomb was considered the first day, and he rose on the third day.

Once the restrictions of the Sabbath day were over, some of Jesus' women disciples went to the tomb. Scholars ponder why they went to anoint a body which had lain dead for almost two full days, and why they went there in the full knowledge that they would not be able to enter the tomb (Mk 16:3). But these details simply underline the miracle of the resurrection: the fact is that Jesus is no longer there.

When they arrive at the tomb, the women are greeted with an extraordinary announcement: 'He has been raised; he is not here. Look, there is the place where they laid him' (16:6). God has not abandoned his obedient Son to the power of death, but raised him to life. This news is too much to take in, and the women are terrified and amazed. This is not all, however, and the person at the empty tomb gives the women a message for the disciples: 'Go, tell his disciples and Peter that he is going ahead of you to Galilee; there you will see him, just as he told you' (16:7).

This is the first message of Jesus after the resurrection. It is one of concern for his disciples, Peter in particular. These are the people who failed him terribly: they all deserted him – Peter denied him. But mercy is at the top of Jesus' post-resurrection agenda. Throughout the Gospel, we have seen the inconsistency of the disciples, and now it seems that Jesus himself is being inconsistent. He does not deliver on his solemn declaration of Mark 8:38, that the Son of Man would be ashamed of those who were ashamed of him. His only thought is of mercy and healing for his followers, and he wishes to meet them in Galilee.

Why Galilee? Jesus began his ministry in Galilee (1:14); it was there that he called his first disciples, including Peter (1:16). He now wishes to lead them back there for a new beginning. Jesus, who has been raised from the dead by his Father, wants to raise his disciples from the death of their infidelity and grief. Galilee is not at the centre of things. It is an insignificant backwater; an unspectacular, marginal place. By inviting the disciples to start there from scratch, Jesus wipes away all the obtuseness and infidelity which they have shown since they first began their discipleship in Galilee. In their walk with Jesus, they appeared to learn nothing. Now, by his mercy, they are forgiven everything. Soon, the power which raised Jesus from the dead will make wise and fearless witnesses of these individuals who have until now excelled only in mediocrity.

For those who study it in depth, one of the greatest riddles of Mark's Gospel is its ending. It seems practically certain that the original manuscript ended with verse 8 of the last chapter,[10] and that the remaining verses were added on a short time later – probably by someone who was taken aback by Mark's very abrupt ending. This does not mean that Mark

16:9-20 is not considered to be inspired. In fact these verses contain nothing that is not found in the other Gospels. But it raises the question of why Mark himself chose to end his Gospel so suddenly, and on a note of uncertainty. If, as seems to be the case, Mark originally ended with the words, 'they said nothing to anyone, for they were afraid', just what had he in mind?

Mark is often quite dramatic, but he is not writing theatre, and feels under no obligation to leave us with a satisfying sense of 'closure'. If we are left with a question mark, this may not be a bad thing. If the question is, 'but what happens next?' then Mark may well have achieved his purpose. The question, 'what happens next?' is always the question of *meditatio*.

Meditatio. How do we wish the Gospel to end? What 'closure' would we like to provide? Is it a 'happily ever after' kind of story? These questions are not about the good news as literature; they are about the Good News as life. Mark did not, in fact, end his Gospel abruptly. He did not end it at all. His audience are invited – quite literally – to draw their own conclusions.

The suddenness of Mark's ending sends *us* to Galilee, along with Peter and the other disciples, to meet the risen Jesus. It is there that we will see him; there, in an old place of new beginnings, we can leave aside our failures and start afresh in our walk with Jesus.

What Jesus brought about by his passion, death and resurrection was *our reconciliation*. As Paul tells us: 'We were reconciled to God through the death of his Son' (Rom 5:10). This reconciliation is not an appearance but a fact. By the mercy of Jesus and the power of the one who raised him from the tomb, we can return to the places from which we have already travelled in failure, and begin again for the very first time. This is Mark's Good News – wonderfully Good News which, far from being repelled by human weakness, lovingly embraces it.

Oratio

Repentance/resolve. Often, Lord, we have hesitated to return to the place of our infidelities and our betrayals, preferring to deny them, to flee from them. Yet it is in returning to our sinfulness, not to dwell on it but to acknowledge it fully and honestly, that we can be completely freed from it. Grant us a knowledge of both our need and your mercy, and with such knowledge, the confidence that we can begin anew, wherever human weakness may have led us. May we experience the freedom which your sacrifice has won for us, and know the peace of the psalmist who prayed: 'I acknowledged my sin to you, and I did not hide my iniquity; I said, "I will confess my transgressions to the Lord", and you forgave the guilt of my sin' (Ps 32:5).

Thanksgiving/praise. We praise you, Lord, God of the impossible, whose love conquers death itself. Because we believe, even the most desperate situations are imbued with hope, and we can say: 'Even though I walk through the darkest valley, I fear no evil; for you are with me' (Ps 23:4). Our own lives are the continuation of the story which you began with the disciples in Galilee. As we walk with you, may we carry in our hearts the prayer of St Paul: 'Thanks be to God, who gives us the victory through our Lord Jesus Christ' (1 Cor 15:57).

Intercession/petition. In your mercy, Lord, let the dawn of the resurrection shine on those who are imprisoned in a tomb of grief, fear or hopelessness. Helped by the compassion of your disciples, may they learn to pray with hope: 'Let me hear of your steadfast love in the morning, for in you I put my trust' (Ps 143:8). May all people come to know your love and mercy, and join in singing your praise: 'Praise the Lord, all you nations! Extol him, all you peoples! For great is his steadfast love toward us, and the faithfulness of the Lord endures forever. Praise the Lord' (Ps 117).

Lectio divina and watchfulness: encouragement from Mark

In our reflections so far, the only chapter of Mark's Gospel to which we have not referred at all is chapter 13. This is quite the strangest chapter in the Gospel, and it uses a lot of the dramatic imagery found in apocalyptic writing (some of which we looked at in our reflection on chapter 13 of the Book of Revelation). In this chapter of Mark, Jesus warns his followers to be on their guard, alert to the challenges that their faith may face in the future. He tells them repeatedly to 'beware,' and to 'keep awake'. Jesus predicts that his return in glory will be preceded by terrible destruction, persecution and a period when people's faith will be put to the test. Because this chapter is all about the future, the time after the resurrection, we can conclude our reflections on Mark by taking from it a future-oriented message for our own discipleship.

Lectio divina is nothing other than attentiveness to God's word; an attentiveness which leads us to live in accordance with that word. Mark 13 is something of a wake-up call, appealing to us to be attentive and alert. During his passion, in the garden of Gethsemane, Jesus appeals to his disciples to 'keep awake' (the repeated command of 13:35 and 37 is mirrored in 14:34 and 38). Jesus does not want his disciples to sleep through any of life's crises, to become dull to his perspective on things, just when that perspective is most critically important. In *lectio divina*, we do nothing other than strive to learn the mind and outlook of God, to be 'renewed in the spirit of our minds' (Eph 4:23). Regular, attentive listening to God's word can gradually, over a lifetime, transform our minds, touching every aspect of our lives and strengthening us for all the challenges of discipleship. Fidelity to times of *lectio divina* will keep us spiritually awake and alert.

We have seen repeatedly that Mark's Gospel speaks in a particular way to those who, for whatever reason, are finding discipleship difficult. As we close our reflections on this Gospel which is so dominated by the cross, we will do well to remember that while Mark's portrayal of discipleship and of Jesus is a 'whole' picture, it is not *the* whole picture. Our reading of Mark should send us to the other portraits of Jesus, which will further deepen our knowledge of Jesus and what it means to be his followers.

NOTES

1. There are several other writings, dating from around the time of the New Testament, which are referred to as Gospels (e.g. the *Gospel of Thomas*). However, they are not considered to be inspired, as are the four biblical or 'canonical' Gospels.

2. This way of summing up the first three stages in *lectio divina* is used by Cardinal Carlo Maria Martini, a biblical scholar and master of *lectio divina*.

3. In other translations, the word 'gospel' may appear here. In Mark's time, this word did not yet refer specifically to the writings which we now call Gospels. The word 'gospel' is a translation of the Greek term which literally means 'good news'.

4. The words Christ and Messiah both mean 'anointed one'. The latter is from the Hebrew; the former from the Greek.

5. The order of the books as they appear in the New Testament is not chronological. Scholars are almost universally agreed that Mark was the earliest Gospel. It was probably written somewhere between 70 and 85 A.D., followed by Matthew a decade or so later. Luke was probably written shortly after Matthew, with John, the last of the four, being written around the end of the first century.

6. The Gospel of John has its own distinctive approach to faith and discipleship. For John, there is a huge contrast between belief and unbelief. While there may be degrees of faith, the most important distinction for John is between unbelievers and believers. It would not have served John's purpose to present the disciples as having no faith. In his language, a disciple with no faith would be a contradiction in terms.

7. The distinction between secular and religious authorities was nowhere near as clear in Jesus' time as it is today, but from a modern perspective, it is accurate enough to place the groups we have mentioned into these categories.

8. In Mark's Greek, these two words are the same.

9. It is often noted that these words are the beginning of a Psalm (Ps 22), which ends on a note of confidence in God. This is true, but there is no doubt that Mark wants us to understand that Jesus reached a point of utter despair on the cross, and a sense of complete abandonment by God.

10. Scholars reach this conclusion on the basis of a careful comparison of the language and style of Mark 16:9-20 with the rest of the Gospel.

Conclusion
Lectio divina at first hand

We began this book by insisting that we can learn to pray only by praying. We will now end by insisting that the only way we can learn to do *lectio divina* is by doing it! Books which 'do' *lectio divina* on particular texts from the Bible can be very helpful – they can stimulate our reflection and give us a desire to become more familiar with the biblical text. But at the end of the day, they cannot really 'do' *lectio divina* for us. Although they can be most helpful, they are, and remain, second hand – someone else's reflections, offered as a help, but no substitute for personal contact with the text.

A temptation for those who study the Bible in depth is to neglect reading the Bible itself, in their concern to read as much as possible of the vast literature *about* the Bible. To do this is to remain at the outskirts of *lectio*, rather like surveying the Promised Land from a distance, instead of entering into it.

Lectio divina invites and helps us to enter into the Scriptures fully, to see in them what we are and what we are called to be. In this ancient but very simple approach to the Bible, we have a reliable guide for our journey towards a transforming encounter with the Lord whose inspired word we read.

Selected passages for *lectio divina*

This short appendix is intended to help readers widen their experience of *lectio divina*. We have seen that even the briefest introduction to a text, or the smallest insight into its background and concerns, can greatly open up what might otherwise remain an obscure passage of Scripture.

What follows is a short selection of passages which have been referred to in the book (other than passages in the Gospel of Mark), along with the relevant page numbers. Reference to these pages may help to stimulate *lectio divina* on the passage concerned.

Genesis 12:1-4, the call of Abraham: pp. 64-67, 82-85, 96-98, 120.

Exodus 3, Moses is commissioned to lead God's people to freedom: p. 27.

Deuteronomy 7:7-8, God's only motivation for entering into relationship with his people is love: p. 36.

1 Kings 19, finding rest and strength in God: p. 28.

Isaiah 1:15-16, the nature of authentic prayer: p. 19.

Is 55:8-9, letting our outlook be changed by God's word: p. 26.

Jeremiah 29:11, hope for the future through trust in God: pp. 22.

Nehemiah 8:1-12, a meditation on praying the word: p. 113.

Matthew 7:24-27, being transformed by God's word: pp. 53, 78, 173.

Luke 4:16-21, God speaks to us now, today: p. 108.

Luke 15:11-32, the parable of the prodigal son: pp. 64, 67-71, 86-89, 98-100.

Luke 24:13-35, Jesus opens the Scriptures to his disciples: pp. 60, 120, 156.

John 5:39-40, an examination of conscience for those who study the Scriptures: p. 51.

2 Timothy 3:16, the Bible is inspired, containing all the wisdom we need: p. 40.

Hebrews 4:12, God's word can read us, shining its light into our lives: pp. 78, 167.

1 John 1:1-2, proclaiming the word with our lives: p. 106.

Revelation 3:20, opening our lives to God: p. 105.

Revelation 13:1-8, fidelity to God – some fearsome biblical imagery: pp. 64, 71-76, 90.

Images of God in the Old and New Testaments (pp. 36-37):

Bridegroom: Hosea 2 and Matthew 25:1-13.

Shepherd: Isaiah 40:11/Psalm 23 and John 15:1-11.

Vinedresser: Isaiah 5:1-7 and John 10:11-18.